OCCASIONAL
PAPER

# The United States, Japan, and Free Trade

Moving in the Same Direction?

Julia F. Lowell, Shujiro Urata, Megumi Naoi, Rachel M. Swanger

Sponsored by The Japan Foundation Center for Global Partnership

CENTER FOR ASIA PACIFIC POLICY

International Programs at RAND

The research described in this report was sponsored by The Japan Foundation Center for Global Partnership and was conducted within the RAND Center for Asia Pacific Policy (CAPP) under the auspices of the International Programs of the RAND Corporation.

**Library of Congress Cataloging-in-Publication Data**

The United States, Japan, and free trade : moving in the same direction? / Julia F. Lowell ... [et al.].
    p. cm.
  Includes bibliographical references.
  ISBN 978-0-8330-6040-2 (pbk. : alk. paper)
  1. United States—Foreign economic relations—Pacific Area. 2. Pacific Area—Foreign economic relations—United States. 3. Japan—Foreign economic relations—Pacific Area. 4. Pacific Area—Foreign economic relations—Japan. 5. United States—Commercial policy. 6. Japan—Commercial policy. I. Lowell, Julia, 1961-

    HF1456.5.P3U55 2012
    382'.710973—dc23

                                                            2012006001

Published 2012 by the RAND Corporation
1776 Main Street, P.O. Box 2138, Santa Monica, CA 90407-2138
1200 South Hayes Street, Arlington, VA 22202-5050
4570 Fifth Avenue, Suite 600, Pittsburgh, PA 15213-2665
RAND URL: http://www.rand.org/
To order RAND documents or to obtain additional information, contact
Distribution Services: Telephone: (310) 451-7002;
Fax: (310) 451-6915; Email: order@rand.org

# Preface

This short assessment of the factors contributing to decisions by the United States and Japan to join the Trans-Pacific Partnership, and what this might mean for bilateral cooperation on trade expansion is part of the RAND Corporation Occasional Paper series. The findings are based on an analysis of interview responses, policy statements, and published and unpublished materials produced by scholars at RAND, Waseda University, and the University of California, San Diego between March 2010 and November 2011. The research was funded by The Japan Foundation Center for Global Partnership, whose mission includes the promotion of scholarly collaboration in order to address issues of global concern.

This research was conducted within the RAND Center for Asia Pacific Policy, part of International Programs at the RAND Corporation. The center aims to improve public policy by providing decisionmakers and the public with rigorous, objective research on critical policy issues affecting Asia and U.S.-Asia relations.

For more information on the RAND Center for Asia Pacific Policy, see http://www.rand.org/international_programs/capp/ or contact the director, Michael Lostumbo, at Michael_Lostumbo@rand.org.

# Contents

# Tables

# Summary

The global trading system is at a turning point. With the Doha Round of trade negotiations floundering, the direction charted by two of the world's largest economies and biggest advocates of unfettered global trade will have a profound impact on the fate of the free trade regime. It was in this context that we launched a project examining whether the United States and Japan could find common ground for cooperation on global trade and, if so, what form that cooperation might take. We looked at four options: (1) working together to restart the multilateral Doha Round of the World Trade Organization (WTO), (2) signing a bilateral free trade agreement (FTA), (3) participating in the formation of the multilateral, regional Trans-Pacific Partnership (TPP), and (4) pursuing independent trade strategies. We evaluated each option based on its impact on international relations and economic growth and its political and practical feasibility.

We found strong evidence supporting the case for cooperation through the TPP. With the announcement on November 7, 2011, by Prime Minister Yoshihiko Noda that Japan would begin discussions to join the TPP, both countries have now committed to negotiations. Whether the United States and Japan will find ways to cooperate to push these negotiations toward a successful conclusion remains to be seen, but our research indicates that this is the best policy option available at this time for both countries. In other words, both the United States and Japan have independently arrived at the decision that joining the TPP is in their own national interest. While this may not guarantee cooperation, we believe it provides solid ground for the two nations to work cooperatively toward a successful conclusion of the TPP.

The benefits of trade liberalization are well established theoretically and empirically. Moreover, the citizens of the United States and Japan have directly experienced and contributed to those benefits over the past 60 years. These economic benefits have derived primarily from multilateral trade liberalization through the General Agreement on Tariffs and Trade (GATT) and its successor regime, the WTO. Therefore, one might assume that these two long-time allies would naturally seek to cooperate in continuing trade liberalization.

Yet, trade also creates pockets of pain as less competitive industries are driven out of business, resulting in lost jobs and, at times, severe hardships for communities. Trade agreements can result in changes to domestic rules and regulations, undermining existing authority and shifting decisionmaking power. Sometimes these shifts produce positive health and safety gains. Sometimes they serve to loosen rules designed to protect the environment and the health and safety of individuals.

This is why trade liberalization is a highly political process that often generates well-organized domestic opposition. Both the United States and Japan face such politicized constituencies, although the supporters and opponents of free trade in each country tend to be mirror opposites. In the United States, labor unions have traditionally been opposed to trade pacts because U.S. manufacturing costs, especially labor costs, are high relative to much of the rest of the world. Farming interests, however, have been aggressively in favor of free trade, albeit opposed to rules that might lead to reduction in their government subsidies, given relatively low costs and high productivity. In Japan, where the reverse cost comparisons typically apply, the most stalwart opponents of free trade have been agricultural interests while business and labor have been generally, if somewhat tepidly, supportive. These differences have made it difficult for the United States and Japan to actively collaborate in pushing the stalled WTO negotiations forward.

Bilateral and regional trade agreements are less desirable than global multilateral agreements because they tend to distort trade, yet beginning with the North American Free Trade Agreement (NAFTA) this is the avenue the United States has been pursuing—partly for economic reasons but also for the diplomatic and political gains that FTAs confer. About a decade later, Japan also joined the game, using FTAs strategically and focusing primarily on Asia. Both countries have exercised their clout in these bilateral agreements to placate domestic opponents of open trade. For instance, environmental and labor force provisions have grown progressively stricter in U.S. FTAs while concessions on agriculture are conspicuously missing from Japan's FTAs. At present, however, neither country finds it politically feasible to engage head-on in a discussion of a U.S.-Japan FTA.

One may ask why we think U.S.-Japan cooperation on trade is possible at this time. The answer is that the economies in the United States and Japan are both in need of outside stimulus to propel them forward. Moreover, both countries are also desirous of maintaining strong leadership positions in Asia. In the case of the United States, the administration of President Barack Obama has launched the National Export Initiative with the goal of doubling the value of U.S. exports by 2015. As part of this effort, President Obama has committed the United States to TPP negotiations. Likewise, Japan has a strong national interest in making sure that it can compete on even footing with both South Korea and China in global markets starting with Asia, and there is growing recognition that if Japan wishes to retain food self-sufficiency, the agricultural sector must attract new investments.

While we believe that it is unlikely that the United States and Japan will find a way to cooperate in reigniting the Doha Round—and that it may not even be possible for them to do so, given strong resistance by large emerging markets such as India and China—we do find ample reasons to believe that both the United States and Japan will move forward with TPP negotiations. By doing so, both countries can strengthen their standing in the Asia-Pacific region and demonstrate a commitment to open markets. This commitment could provide at least a temporary economic boost and, if the TPP fulfills its promise to be comprehensive and broad-based, it should generate significant longer-term stimulus. Opposition to the TPP in the United States has been muted in part because it has had a relatively low profile. The addition of Japan will raise the profile and the stakes, but it will also increase the potential gains. Conversely, Japan faced vociferous and fervent opposition prior to Prime Minister Noda's announcement, but this may diminish over time as the outlines of the scope of expected concessions as well as benefits become clearer.

# Acknowledgments

We would like to thank individuals currently or formerly employed by the following organizations for their help with our research: the Japan-America Society of Southern California; Japan Broadcasting Corporation; the Consulate General of Japan in Los Angeles; the Japan Federation of Business (Keidanren); the Ministry of Economy, Trade and Industry; the Ministry of Foreign Affairs; Keizai Koho Center; the Office of the U.S. Trade Representative; the Port of Los Angeles; the U.S.-Japan Business Council; Meiji University; the U.S. State Department; the University of California, San Diego; and Waseda University.

We are particularly grateful to Saori Katada, Associate Professor at the School of International Relations, University of Southern California, and Charles Wolf, Distinguished Chair in International Economics at RAND, for their many helpful comments and suggestions on how to improve the paper. We also thank Yashodara Rana and Zhimin Mao, graduate students at the Pardee RAND Graduate School, who provided useful assistance with parts of the research. Finally, deep and sincere thanks to The Japan Foundation Center for Global Partnership in New York and Tokyo, which made this study possible.

# Abbreviations

| | |
|---|---|
| APEC | Asia-Pacific Economic Cooperation |
| ASEAN | Association of Southeast Asian Nations |
| CAFTA-DR | Dominican Republic–Central America–U.S. Free Trade Agreement |
| DPJ | Democratic Party of Japan |
| EPA | economic partnership agreement |
| FDI | foreign direct investment |
| FTA | free trade agreement |
| FTAA | Free Trade Area of the Americas |
| FTAAP | Free Trade Area of the Asia Pacific |
| GATT | General Agreement on Tariffs and Trade |
| GDP | gross domestic product |
| IMF | International Monetary Fund |
| KORUS FTA | Republic of Korea–United States Free Trade Agreement |
| LDP | Liberal Democratic Party |
| MAFF | Ministry of Agriculture, Fishery and Forestry |
| MEFTA | Middle East Free Trade Agreement |
| MENA | Middle Eastern-North African |
| METI | Ministry of Economy, Trade, and Industry |
| MoFA | Ministry of Foreign Affairs |
| NAFTA | North American Free Trade Agreement |
| OECD | Organisation for Economic Co-operation and Development |
| TAA | trade adjustment assistance |
| TPA | trade promotion agreement |

TPP                Trans-Pacific Partnership
UAW                United Auto Workers
US-SACU FTA        U.S.-Southern Africa Customs Union Free Trade Agreement
USTR               U.S. Trade Representative
WTO                World Trade Organization

# CHAPTER ONE

# Introduction

On November 7, 2011, Japanese Prime Minister Yoshihiko Noda announced that Japan would explore participation in the Trans-Pacific Partnership (TPP), a proposed regional free trade agreement (FTA) involving nine Asia-Pacific countries.[1] Joining the TPP could represent a significant step for Japan, which up until now has avoided any negotiations that might require it to liberalize its heavily protected agricultural markets. A key feature of the TPP has been the participants' insistence on eliminating all tariffs—with very few exceptions.[2]

The United States has cautiously welcomed Japan's decision to join the TPP negotiations, although U.S. government officials have made it clear that this decision was Japan's alone and not in response to any U.S. pressure. They have also indicated that they expect Japan to meet the "high standards" of liberalized trade the pact is aiming for. Japanese participation in the pact is important to the United States because Japan is its fourth largest trading partner and a key player in the Asia-Pacific regional economy. On the other hand, Japanese participation may make it more difficult to sell the pact to U.S. interest groups that doubt Japan's commitment to liberalization.

This paper examines the factors that influenced Japan's decision to join the TPP and the U.S. decision to make the TPP a focus of its trade policy. It does so in the context of four trade policy options that were available to the two countries as of the beginning of November 2011: (1) working together to restart the multilateral Doha Round of the World Trade Organization (WTO), (2) signing a bilateral FTA, (3) participating in the TPP, and (4) continuing with their own independent trade strategies. We assess each option based on its ability to achieve broad objectives common to U.S. and Japanese policymakers, informing our assessment with an analysis of the economic and political environments in which the policymakers were operating prior to Japan's TPP decision. Specifically, for each country we consider to what extent the hypothesized policies were likely to

- strengthen its international reputation and relations
- stimulate the economy in the short run
- promote long-run economic growth
- achieve broad political acceptability at home
- allow implementation notwithstanding domestic and international political and economic constraints.

---

[1] Subsequent to Japan's announcement, Canada and Mexico also formally expressed interest in joining the TPP negotiations (Garibian and Younglai, 2011).

[2] Some exclusions that are allowed under preexisting bilateral FTAs may also be allowed under the TPP (Associated Press, 2011).

This study draws on published and unpublished research as well as interviews in Tokyo and Washington, D.C., and discussions at RAND, Waseda University, and the University of California, San Diego held between March 2010 and November 2011. The study was supported by the The Japan Foundation Center for Global Partnership, an independent agency funded by the Japanese government to promote scholarly collaboration between Japan and the United States.

We begin the paper by providing an overview of the origin and status of the TPP negotiations. We then briefly describe the benefits of multilateral, bilateral, and regional trade liberalization, explaining why, despite these benefits, liberalization often attracts strong domestic opposition. Next, we identify some of the features of the economic and political environments that serve as opportunities and constraints for policymakers. Characterizing each of the policy options, we evaluate them according to the criteria listed above. Our conclusion is that, given the prevailing policy environments in both countries, U.S.-Japanese cooperation through the TPP appears to have the greatest potential to move both countries forward on freeing trade. The choice by both countries to move forward with the TPP is therefore justified on these grounds.

# CHAPTER TWO

# The Trans-Pacific Partnership

The Trans-Pacific Partnership (TPP) is intended to be a comprehensive regional trade agreement that deepens economic ties among its members by opening up trade in goods and services, boosting investment flows, and promoting closer links across a range of economic policy and regulatory issues. A key focus of the agreement is to serve as a building block toward the longer term goal of a Free Trade Area of the Asia Pacific (FTAAP) encompassing all 21 members of APEC (the Asia-Pacific Economic Cooperation forum). Asia-Pacific countries are encouraged to join in the agreement, although consensus among the current parties to the negotiations is required in order for a new member to join. The nine countries currently committed to negotiation are Australia, Brunei Darussalam, Chile, Malaysia, New Zealand, Peru, Singapore, the United States, and Vietnam. As of November 2011, three additional Asia-Pacific countries—Japan, Canada, and Mexico—have publically expressed an interest in joining.

The TPP grew out of the Pacific Three Closer Economic Partnership, or "P3," an FTA between Chile, New Zealand, and Singapore that was launched in 2002.[1] When Brunei Darussalam asked to join as a founding member before the final round of negotiations in April 2005, the pact was renamed the Trans-Pacific Strategic Economic Partnership Agreement, or "P4." From the very beginning, the goal of the P4 was to develop a comprehensive model agreement that would attract new Asia-Pacific members. In November 2009, the P4 partners plus the United States, Australia, Peru, and Vietnam announced that they would begin formal negotiations on a new agreement that would expand on the P4: the TPP.

As with the P4, the TPP negotiations cover market access for trade in goods (customs procedures, rules of origin, technical barriers to trade, etc.), trade in services, government procurement, intellectual property, competition policy, and dispute settlement (Capling, 2009). Unlike the P4, the TPP will also cover cross-border trade in financial services and provide substantive legal protections for investors and investments. In August 2010, the Office of the U.S. Trade Representative (USTR) announced that all of the TPP participants, regardless of developmental level, have also agreed to establish common minimum labor and environmental standards. Further cross-cutting issues under negotiation include regulatory coherence, supply chain management, trade facilitation, and border issues (Fergusson and Vaughn, 2010; USTR, 2011). By November 2011, the original nine TPP participating countries had completed nine rounds of negotiations.

---

[1]  The P3 had its origins in a 1998 U.S. proposal for the negotiation of an FTA between Australia, New Zealand, Chile, Singapore, and the United States. According to Capling (2009), the proposal was intended to spur Asian members of the APEC into action on trade liberalization.

In sum, the TPP is intended to be a comprehensive, "high quality" FTA that substantively broadens and deepens the economic integration of the Asia-Pacific region. As such, it is almost certain to generate strong domestic support and opposition in the countries that are its prospective signatories—as discussed in the following chapter.

# CHAPTER THREE

# The Effects of Trade Liberalization

**Trade liberalization helps the economy.** The arguments for trade liberalization are well known, but worth repeating:

- Trade spurs competition, motivating businesses to develop new products, find new production processes and technologies, and advance knowledge.
- Consumers as a whole gain from increased choice and better goods and services at lower prices.
- Investors in competitive industries receive higher returns due to expanded markets and lower production costs.
- Countries as a whole benefit from higher employment and higher growth rates due to the greater innovation and higher productivity spurred by foreign competition.
- Countries as a whole benefit also from the higher employment and higher growth obtained from export expansion when their trading partners' markets are liberalized.

**The benefits of freer trade are not distributed evenly.** Despite these clear benefits, countries rarely choose to remove barriers to trade unilaterally. There is often significant opposition to trade agreements, whether they occur in the multilateral context of the WTO or in the bilateral or plurilateral contexts of FTAs. The primary reason is that trade liberalization has distributional consequences, creating losers as well as winners. While consumers, investors, and workers in competitive domestic firms almost always benefit from trade liberalization, some domestic firms—typically those with higher costs or less attractive products than their foreign competitors—may lose or be driven out of business, with consequent loss of jobs and profitability. Under certain conditions, increased trade also has the potential to damage the natural environment (depending on local laws and trade agreement provisions), reduce food and military security, and worsen domestic and international labor conditions.[1] Would-be liberalizers, therefore, must take steps to mitigate these kinds of negative impacts in order to overcome domestic opposition.

**Trade opponents are well organized.** In fact, would-be liberalizers must work within a political process in which trade opponents are often better organized than trade advocates. One reason is that the effects of liberalization on less-competitive producer groups tend to be concentrated and adverse, whereas the effects on consumers and investors are more positive. But because the positive effects are widely shared among disparate groups, they have less power

---

[1]  For an analysis of the potential environmental impacts of trade, both positive and negative, see, for example, Gallagher (2008) and Harris (2004). For an analysis of the links between trade and national security, see Neu and Wolf (1994). For an analysis of the links between trade and labor conditions, see, for example, Rodrik (1997).

to galvanize action. Within producer groups, opponents often have more political power than advocates because potential job and income losses worry elected officials more than potential job and income gains excite them. This is understandable, since the size and location of job and income losses are often predictable while the size and location of gains are much more uncertain. In addition, single-issue nongovernmental organizations, such as environmental and labor groups, are growing increasingly influential. In Japan, the strongest resistance to liberalization typically comes from agricultural producers. In the United States, the strongest resistance tends to come from environmental groups, labor unions, and less-competitive producers in such industries as automobiles, steel, and textiles. In both countries, individual industry and even individual company positions on FTAs vary from agreement to agreement, depending on the proposed partner country and industries involved.

**Comprehensive multilateral liberalization is best.** Preferential agreements tend to distort patterns of trade, disadvantaging producers located in nonmember countries even when they have the best or lowest-priced product. It is therefore generally agreed that multilateral liberalization brings more benefits than preferential liberalization. Nevertheless, a growing number of countries are choosing to pursue bilateral and regional FTAs rather than focusing their efforts on ensuring a successful Doha Round. The reasons for the switch to FTAs include the improved ability to

- find common ground with a smaller and less diverse set of countries
- leave highly politically sensitive sectors off the table
- exclude entire countries that are perceived to be too competitive across a broad range of politically sensitive sectors
- keep up the momentum of trade liberalization while the Doha Round is stalled.

**FTAs that most closely approximate fully multilateral free trade raise global welfare the most.** FTAs vary according to the number and nature of their members, their market coverage, and their rules of origin. All else equal, FTAs that have many members, that have large economies as members, and that have broad market coverage tend to raise global welfare the most because they penalize exports from nonmember countries the least. Thus, to the extent that they include more producers that are highly competitive, large regional FTAs are preferable to bilateral FTAs. For the same reason, FTAs with broad market coverage and nonrestrictive rules of origin are the most liberalizing because they are the least distortionary. For example, in the case where rules of origin are nonpreferential, nonmember exporters can ship to whichever FTA member imposes the lowest tariff on their products and then transship them to the other FTA members with no additional tax penalty. As long as the costs associated with transshipment are not too high, consumers throughout the FTA will benefit. In practice, however, most FTAs—including most regional FTAs—exclude significant sectors (such as agriculture) from liberalization and also maintain highly restrictive rules of origin. On purely economic grounds, therefore, they are inferior to multilateral free trade.

# CHAPTER FOUR

# The U.S. Economic Policy Environment

## The Status of the U.S. Economy

**The United States remains on the edge of recession.** In 2007, the U.S. economy slowed down in response to a collapse of the housing market. By the end of 2008, the downturn had developed into a full-blown financial crisis and the "Great Recession" had spread to the rest of the world. Between 2007 and 2010, the average unemployment rate in the United States rose from 4.6 to 9.6 percent, and there were some notable bankruptcies, including Lehman Brothers, Washington Mutual, General Motors, and Chrysler. During the worst of the crisis, in the fourth quarter of 2008, U.S. economic output fell by almost 9 percent.[1] Since then unemployment has come down a bit, and economic growth has stabilized—though it remains lackluster. U.S. policymakers continue to be concerned about the potential for a "double-dip" recession, as recent European financial troubles are being translated into declines in European demand for U.S. products (Elliott, 2011).

**High levels of government borrowing pose a growing threat to the U.S. economy.** Policymakers are also very concerned about the gross general government debt, which in 2011 was predicted to reach almost 100 percent of gross domestic product (GDP) (IMF, 2011).[2] Although this percentage is not wildly out of line relative to other advanced industrialized countries (Canadian gross government debt is expected to reach 84 percent of GDP in 2011, for example, while the debt-to-GDP ratio for countries in the Euro area as a whole is 89 percent), it is nevertheless of enormous concern. One reason is that, in absolute terms, it is a large amount for world debt markets to absorb—$13.5 trillion in 2010—and it has more than doubled over the past ten years. A second reason is that interest payments on the debt are rising and are likely to rise even more quickly now that a major rating agency has removed the United States from its list of "AAA" or least-risky borrowers. A third reason, which may be the most important of the three, is that almost half of publicly held U.S. government debt is held by foreigners. Should these investors lose confidence in the government's ability to pay them back, it is likely that domestic interest rates will shoot up, the dollar exchange rate will plummet, or some combination of the two will occur. The implications for U.S. residents would be higher inflation, tighter credit, a lower growth rate, and higher unemployment.

---

[1]  Authors' calculations based on data from the U.S. Census Bureau (2012) and U.S. Bureau of Economic Analysis (undated-b).

[2]  This figure includes debt issued by federal, state, and local governments and debt held in the banking system and by government agencies; it does not net out financial assets, such as monetary gold, currency, or debt securities held by governments.

**U.S. policymakers see exports as a crucial source of growth.** Most of the economies in East Asia (though not Japan), South Asia, Latin America, and even sub-Saharan Africa have already rebounded from the Great Recession of 2007–2010. China and India, in particular, although not without serious problems, are going strong, achieving annual real GDP growth rates of 10.4 percent and 8.8 percent, respectively, in 2010 (World Bank, 2011). In light of the spectacular meltdown of U.S. financial and housing markets in 2008–2009, high domestic unemployment, and the resultant ballooning of the U.S government budget deficit, U.S. policymakers are very concerned about the prospects for growth in the U.S. domestic components of demand (consumption, investment, and government spending). They believe that greater access to strong external markets could spur exports and so boost the struggling U.S. economy and prepare the way for stronger future growth. With the exception of one down year (2009), a strong upward trend in U.S. exports as a share of GDP since 2003 supports this view.

**Services account for most U.S. economic activity, followed by a diversified goods-producing sector.** Services accounted for more than three-quarters of U.S. economic activity in 2010, followed by the nonfarm goods-producing sector (22 percent) and the agricultural sector (1 percent). Within the goods-producing sector, manufacturing is the largest contributor to GDP at 12 percent.[3] On the employment front in 2010, total service-sector jobs represented almost 90 percent of all nonfarm employment, led by government, education, and health services and retail trade. Services accounted for more than 80 percent of all private nonfarm employment.[4] Most of these jobs are provided by businesses that employ fewer than five people on a full- or part-time basis.[5]

**Services represent a growing share of U.S. exports.** In 2010, the total value of U.S. merchandise exports was second only to those of China (8.4 percent as opposed to 10.4 percent of world merchandise exports), whereas the total value of U.S. service exports far outstripped that of the second biggest service exporter, Germany (14.1 percent as opposed to 6.3 percent of world service exports). Over the past decade, service exports have grown faster than merchandise exports (average annual rate of 7 percent as opposed to 6 percent), and have also proved more resistant to recession: Between 2007 and 2009, exports of merchandise goods fell by 14 percent, but exports of services actually grew by 3 percent (USITA, 2011).

**Asian countries account for a growing share of U.S. trade.** Among the top U.S. export partners over the last decade (countries where the total ten-year value of exports exceeded $100 billion), nine out of nineteen were in the Asia-Pacific region.[6] Over the same period, India, China, Hong Kong, South Korea, and Singapore accounted for six of the top ten fastest-growing U.S. export markets (USITA, 2011).

**The United States is a major agricultural exporter—and subsidizer.** The United States is the top agricultural exporter in the world, followed by Canada, Brazil, China, and Australia. (If the European Union is considered as one country, it takes top spot.) The top five U.S. agricultural exports are grains and feeds, soybeans, red meats and products, tree nuts and preparations, and animal feeds and oil meal (WTO, 2010a). According to the Organisation

---

[3]   Authors' calculation based on data from the U.S. Bureau of Economic Analysis (undated-b).

[4]   Authors' calculation based on data from the U.S. Department of Labor (2012).

[5]   Does not include self-employment, which accounts for roughly one in nine U.S. workers (Hipple, 2010).

[6]   Authors' calculations based on data from the U.S. Census Bureau (2012). The top Asian export destinations were China, Japan, Korea, Taiwan, Singapore, Hong Kong, Australia, India, and Malaysia.

for Economic Co-operation and Development (OECD), U.S. agricultural exports are also among the most heavily subsidized, although—since most of the subsidies are decoupled from current production and provided instead as income support—they are less trade distortionary. The United States was just behind the European Union, and just ahead of Japan, Korea, and Switzerland in terms of the total value of direct export subsidies, including both distorting and nondistorting government support for agriculture (OECD, 2011).

**Asian countries are underrepresented in U.S. direct investment flows.** The United States is both the largest foreign direct investor in the world and the largest recipient of such funds. According to the U.S. Bureau of Economic Analysis, by the end of 2010, U.S. firms had accumulated $3.9 trillion worth of direct investment abroad on a historical cost basis, compared with $2.3 trillion acquired by foreign investors in the United States.[7] Within the United States, in 2008 U.S. multinationals produced goods and services that made up about 21 percent of U.S. GDP and were among the largest firms by employment (Barefoot and Mataloni, 2010). Cumulatively, the countries with the largest amount of U.S. direct investment as of 2010 were the Netherlands, the United Kingdom, and Canada. On a flow basis, the top three targets for U.S. investment were the United Kingdom, the Netherlands, and Luxembourg. Asian countries are somewhat low on the list relative to their prominence as trading partners: In 2010, China was ninth among recipients of U.S. direct investment abroad, Japan was 11th, and South Korea was 24th.[8]

## The Evolution of U.S. Trade Policy

**The first U.S. free trade agreements were not primarily about liberalizing trade.** The United States has long been one of the staunchest supporters of the multilateral trading system—at least in principle. The United States was a leader in the formation of the General Agreement on Tariffs and Trade (GATT) and its subsequent liberalization rounds and pushed hard for the Uruguay Round and the 1995 creation of the WTO. It did not enter into its first FTA until 1985, with Israel, which it followed four years later with the Canada-U.S. Free Trade Agreement. After a significant hiatus, U.S. policymakers then supported the transformation of the Canada-U.S. agreement into the North American Free Trade Agreement (NAFTA) in 1994. Over this period, U.S. policymakers appear to have viewed preferential trade deals primarily as a means for putting pressure on global trade talks and as foreign policy instruments. Their main focus remained the multilateral WTO (Rosen, 2004; Schott, 2004; Lawrence, 2006).

**The number of FTAs grew rapidly in the 2000s.** The decade of the 2000s, however, saw the evolution of a new U.S. trade policy approach as NAFTA's success contrasted with the WTO's failure to achieve U.S. liberalization and market access objectives. As shown in Table 1, between January 2000 and October 2011 the United States signed FTAs with 17 countries, including South Korea, Colombia, and Panama; implemented 14 of them, and joined in on negotiations for the TPP, which will potentially create FTA partnerships with four new coun-

---

[7]    Data from the U.S. Bureau of Economic Analysis (undated-a).

[8]    Data from the U.S. Bureau of Economic Analysis (undated-a).

**Table 1**
**U.S. Free Trade Agreements by Partner**

| Partner | FTA Name | Date Signed (President) | Date Ratified by Congress (President) | Date in Effect |
|---|---|---|---|---|
| Negotiations concluded or in progress | | | | |
| Israel | US-Israel FTA | April 1985 (Reagan) | August 1985 (Reagan) | September 1985 |
| Canada | CUSFTA[a] | January 1988 (Reagan) | September 1985 (Reagan) | January 1989 |
| | NAFTA[b] | October 1992 (Bush I) | November 1993 (Clinton) | January 1994 |
| Mexico | NAFTA | October 1992 (Bush I) | November 1993 (Clinton) | January 1994 |
| Jordan | US-Jordan FTA | October 2000 (Clinton) | September 2001 (Bush II) | January 2001 |
| Chile | US-Chile FTA | June 2003 (Bush II) | July 2003 (Bush II) | January 2004 |
| | TPP[c] | Talks in progress | | |
| Singapore | US-Singapore FTA | May 2003 (Bush II) | July 2003 (Bush II) | January 2004 |
| | TPP | Talks in progress | | |
| Australia | AUSFTA | May 2004 (Bush II) | July 2004 (Bush II) | January 2005 |
| | TPP | Talks in progress | | |
| Bahrain | US-Bahrain FTA | September 2004 (Bush II) | December 2005 (Bush II) | January 2006 |
| Morocco | US-Morocco FTA | June 2004 (Bush II) | July 2004 (Bush II) | January 2006 |
| El Salvador | CAFTA-DR[d] | August 2004 (Bush II) | July 2005 (Bush II) | March 2006 |
| Honduras | CAFTA-DR | August 2004 (Bush II) | July 2005 (Bush II) | April 2006 |
| Nicaragua | CAFTA-DR | August 2004 (Bush II) | July 2005 (Bush II) | April 2006 |
| Guatemala | CAFTA-DR | August 2004 (Bush II) | July 2005 (Bush II) | July 2006 |
| Dominican Rep. | CAFTA-DR | August 2004 (Bush II) | July 2005 (Bush II) | March 2007 |
| Costa Rica | CAFTA-DR | August 2004 (Bush II) | July 2005 (Bush II) | January 2009 |
| Oman | US-Oman FTA | January 2006 (Bush II) | September 2006 (Bush II) | January 2009 |
| Peru | US-Peru TPA | April 2006 (Bush II) | December 2007 (Bush II) | February 2009 |
| | TPP | Talks in progress | | |
| Colombia | US-Colombia FTA | November 2006 (Bush II) | October 2011 (Obama) | TBD |
| S. Korea | KORUS FTA[e] | June 2007 (Bush II) | October 2011 (Obama) | TBD |
| Panama | US-Panama FTA | June 2007 (Bush II) | October 2011 (Obama) | TBD |
| Brunei | TPP | Negotiations in progress | | |
| New Zealand | TPP | Negotiations in progress | | |
| Malaysia | TPP | Negotiations in progress | | |
| Vietnam | TPP | Negotiations in progress | | |

**Table 1—Continued**

| Partner | FTA Name | Date Signed (President) | Date Ratified by Congress (President) | Date in Effect |
|---|---|---|---|---|
| Negotiations suspended | | | | |
| 34 countries | FTAA[f] | Suspended | | |
| Thailand | US-Thailand FTA | Suspended | | |
| Ecuador | Andean-US FTA | Suspended | | |
| Malaysia | US-Malaysia FTA | Converted to TPP | | |
| SACU[g] | US-SACU FTA | Terminated | | |

SOURCE: USTR, undated.

[a] Canada-U.S. Free Trade Agreement.

[b] North American Free Trade Agreement.

[c] Trans-Pacific Partnership.

[d] Dominican Republic–Central America–U.S. Free Trade Agreement.

[e] Korea–U.S. Free Trade Agreement.

[f] Free Trade Area of the Americas.

[g] Southern African Customs Union (SACU) members are Botswana, Lesotho, Namibia, South Africa, and Swaziland.

tries and deepen commitments to four existing FTA partners.[9] Of the 20 FTAs that the United States has signed with individual countries, 12 have been with Western Hemisphere partners, five with Middle Eastern-North African (MENA) partners, and three with Asia-Pacific partners. By far the most significant of these, in terms of the value of trade involved, is the NAFTA agreement with Canada and Mexico. In 2011, Canada and Mexico together accounted for approximately 26 percent of U.S. imports and 33 percent of U.S. exports. Outside of NAFTA, the largest U.S. FTA partner economy is Singapore, which in 2011 accounted for approximately 1 percent of U.S. imports and 2 percent of U.S. exports.[10]

**FTAs are becoming the primary instrument of U.S. trade policy—but most are not economically significant.** The growth in the number of U.S. FTAs since 1985—and especially since 2000—suggests that preferential arrangements are no longer simply a sideshow for U.S. trade policy but are well on their way to becoming the main act. Nevertheless, with the exception of NAFTA, it appears that up to now economic goals have not been paramount in U.S. FTA formation. Individually, most of the United States' current FTA partners are quite small, and do not offer any unique advantages in terms of industrial capabilities or natural resources. And although East Asia is one of the fastest growing regions in the world, only three of the U.S. FTAs involve Asian countries (see Table 1). The FTA with Korea represents a much more significant commitment to liberalization through preferential trade. But without admitting new partners, such as Japan, the TPP will not provide much of a spark to an export-led U.S. recovery.

---

[9]   In addition, talks to establish a Free Trade Area of the Americas (FTAA) involved 34 countries; another proposed FTA with the U.S.-Southern Africa Customs Union (US-SACU FTA) involved six countries. The FTAA talks were suspended in 2005; the US-SACU FTA was scaled back to a Trade and Investment Cooperation Agreement in 2008 (Jackson, 2009).

[10]   Authors' calculations based on data from the U.S. Census Bureau (2012).

**Foreign policy considerations continue to be important determinants of U.S. FTAs.** The pattern of U.S. FTA formation over time suggests that, in many cases, foreign policy goals continue to drive the choice of partner for U.S. FTAs. Early FTAs with Israel and Jordan, for example, were likely motivated by the desire to reward those countries' efforts toward achieving Middle East peace (Rosen, 2006). More-recent FTAs with Bahrain, Morocco, and Oman were part of President George W. Bush's Middle East Free Trade (MEFTA) initiative, which was designed to strengthen strategic relationships with moderate Muslim countries in the Middle East in the wake of the September 2011 terrorist attacks (Momani, 2007; USGAO, 2007). FTAs with Singapore and Australia were also likely motivated primarily by security considerations: the first as a reward for Singapore's willingness to provide the U.S. military with access to bases in Southeast Asia when U.S. air and naval bases in the Philippines were closed down in 1991; the second as a reward to Australia for supporting the U.S. invasion of Iraq in 2003 (Pang, 2007; Siracusa, 2006).

**Relative to most other countries' FTAs, U.S. FTAs are comprehensive in their coverage.** With the exception of the very first FTA with Israel, the U.S. FTA agenda has been quite ambitious. It has focused prominently on the "WTO-plus" issues of expanding trade in services, opening up government procurement to foreign competition, eliminating technical barriers to trade, increasing foreign investment (foreign direct investment [FDI] and portfolio) and protecting intellectual property rights. Since 2001, each U.S. FTA has also included chapters that deal with a number of additional issues, such as opening up agricultural markets, reducing government subsidies, boosting cross-border investment, harmonizing competition policy, and ensuring environmental safeguards and labor standards. In general, U.S. FTAs take a "negative list" approach to liberalization, meaning that the partners commit to opening all sectors except those explicitly identified as exceptions; this contrasts with the WTO "positive list" approach, in which signatories commit to opening only those sectors that they single out for liberalization. All U.S. FTAs also incorporate their own dispute resolution mechanisms, which in many cases include "choice of forum" provisions whereby the complaining party is allowed to choose whether to bring action through the FTA or take it to the WTO's Dispute Settlement Body (Schott, 2004; Jackson, 2009; Lord, 2010).

**Beginning with NAFTA, the environmental and labor force provisions of U.S. FTAs have gotten progressively stricter.** In the original version of NAFTA, President George H.W. Bush included measures designed to uphold national environmental, health, and labor standards and to encourage the upward harmonization of those standards across the three partner countries. When these measures failed to satisfy politically powerful critics of the pact, two side accords with stronger provisions protecting labor and the environment were negotiated by the Clinton administration. These were enough to win approval for NAFTA, and following this success, these stricter provisions—including the creation of formal and informal institutions and procedures for furthering labor and environmental goals—became standard. The passage of these accords has convinced some but not all environmental groups that NAFTA could actually strengthen rather than weaken North American environmental protections (Higley and Sutton, 1992; Mumme, 1999; Gantz, 2011).

**U.S. FTAs still contain a number of protectionist measures.** Nevertheless, a number of restrictions and protectionist measures still prevail in U.S. FTAs. For example, under NAFTA, the rules of origin for imported clothing require that the raw material (fiber), cloth, and final garment all be manufactured within the United States, Canada, or Mexico. In the case of the U.S.-Australia FTA, sugar was left off the table entirely, while strict quotas limiting duty-free access to the American beef, dairy, peanut, cotton, and tobacco markets were scheduled to be phased out as long as 18 years after the agreement was passed. Cross-sectoral protectionist measures, including government subsidies, and "trade remedies" such as antidumping penalties, countervailing duties, and various types of safeguards against import surges, are also generally allowed in U.S. FTAs, provided they do not violate WTO rules (WTO, 2010a).

# CHAPTER FIVE

# The U.S. Political Environment

## U.S. Trade Politics—Actors and Issues

**The Obama administration sees trade agreements as a means of promoting U.S. exports.** President Obama pushed for the conclusion of all three of the FTAs initiated by former president George W. Bush and formally entered the United States into negotiations for the TPP. The Obama administration sees the opening of foreign markets—whether through trade pacts or the National Export Initiative (an export-promotion strategy with the goal of doubling the value of U.S. exports by 2015)—as a way to boost the U.S. economy. The downsides to trade liberalization, such as possible foreign environmental degradation and job losses due to import competition, are being handled as they have been by past administrations—through environmental protection provisions, long lead times, and trade adjustment assistance (TAA) to workers adversely affected by trade agreements.

**Republican leaders agreed to support free trade pacts with Colombia, Panama, and South Korea although they opposed reauthorization of TAA.** Republicans have traditionally been the party of trade liberalization, but the strongest group within the party today is the "Tea Party," which has no declared position on trade but a strong commitment to deficit reduction and smaller government. Since reauthorization of TAA will contribute to the budget deficit—and since its effectiveness is disputed—many Republicans initially declared they would not support the FTAs with Colombia, Panama, and South Korea unless TAA were excluded. Under pressure from pro-trade business groups, however, in September 2011 Republican leaders agreed to pass a slightly scaled-back version of TAA. On October 12, all three trade pacts were ratified by Congress, with especially strong bipartisan support for KORUS. Passage of KORUS was a top priority for U.S. agricultural interests, particularly the beef, poultry, wheat, and soybean industries.

**Most U.S. labor unions remain strongly opposed to trade liberalization—but there are exceptions.** Labor unions are among the strongest and most vocal opponents of trade liberalization in the United States. Since the 1980s, labor leaders have opposed almost every initiative that might threaten U.S. jobs due to increased imports—including NAFTA, CAFTA-DR, China's entry into the WTO, and the original trade agreements with Colombia, Korea, and Panama signed by President George W. Bush (Griswold, 2010). In an important departure from the past, however, the United Auto Workers (UAW) and the United Food and Commercial Workers have both come out in favor of the revised Korea pact negotiated by Obama in December 2010. The UAW agreed to support the revised agreement because it believed that KORUS is the best deal it can hope for in the current political environment. The revised KORUS extends the number of years the U.S. can impose tariffs on imported vehicles and

15

opens the South Korean market to U.S. cars by eliminating and reducing Korean tariffs on U.S. vehicles and trucks (Rummel, 2010).

**Opposition to FTAs among U.S. environmental groups has diminished.** When NAFTA was signed in October 1992 by President George H.W. Bush, opposition from U.S. environmental groups was nearly unanimous—despite the fact that the agreement included unprecedented measures designed to uphold national environmental standards. In the face of NAFTA's politically powerful critics, President Bill Clinton negotiated two side accords, one on labor and one on the environment. While not all environmental groups are convinced, the passage of these accords has persuaded a number of them that, with careful negotiation, FTAs could actually strengthen rather than weaken U.S. environmental protections.[1]

**U.S. policymakers would like to create a Free Trade Agreement of the Asia Pacific, both to offset China's rising influence in the region and to ensure that the United States retains the ability to export there.** The proliferation of preferential trading agreements in Asia has worried U.S. policymakers. In particular, China has been especially active in forming FTAs with countries in the fast-growing Asia-Pacific region. By mid-2011, China had completed 11 FTAs and was in the process of negotiating another 13, including a completed FTA with the Association of Southeast Asian Nations (ASEAN) and a proposed FTA with Japan and South Korea (Zhang and Shen, 2011). U.S. policymakers have expressed support for a pan-Asian FTA that would eventually include China but not until issues such as regulatory cooperation and standards for workers' rights and the environment have already been decided. They view the TPP as an important step to achieving a broader FTAAP (Bergsten, 2007).

**Rebalancing U.S. foreign policy energy and resources toward the Asia-Pacific Region is a stated policy of the Obama Administration.** Although comprehensive trade agreements are notoriously difficult to negotiate and consequently prone to be dropped from foreign policy agendas in favor of more pressing and compelling issues, for now, TPP appears to be in a policy sweet spot. It intersects with a number of key priorities for the Obama administration, including (1) rebalancing U.S. foreign policy toward the Asia-Pacific region and (2) enhancing U.S. economic statecraft by using diplomacy to strengthen the domestic economy and using economic tools to address foreign policy challenges.[2] But it could easily get swept off the list of policy priorities should a confrontation with Iran, for instance, develop. Even short of a foreign policy crisis, given that 2012 is an election year, President Obama or members of his administration may decide that their limited political capital would be better deployed to achieving a policy objective that is less controversial and a higher priority for a core constituency.

---

[1]  Seven environmental groups that supported the NAFTA side agreements were the World Wildlife Fund, National Wildlife Federation, National Resources Defense Council, Environmental Defense Fund, Defenders of Wildlife, Conservation International, and the Audubon Society (Hufbauer and Schott, 2005).

[2]  Secretary Clinton laid this out in a speech to the Economic Club of New York in October 2011. Matthew Goodman, Senior Economic Advisor, Department of State also discussed it at a panel discussion on the Trans-Pacific Partnership held at the Center for Strategic and International Studies, January 4, 2012.

# CHAPTER SIX

# The Japanese Economic Policy Environment

## The Status of the Japanese Economy

**Japan has never fully recovered from the collapse of the 1980s "bubble economy."**[1] In 1990, the Japanese stock market crashed, followed by a collapse in the commercial real estate market. This marked the beginning of a decade of slow-to-no-growth and deflationary pressure, which in the 2000s evolved into a succession of weak recoveries alternating with economic downturns. When the global financial crisis first hit in 2008, the initial impact on Japan was fairly small because Japanese banks had relatively little exposure to U.S. mortgage markets (Sato, 2009). However, the resulting global recession hit Japanese exports hard, having the effect of weak overseas demand exacerbated by a strengthening yen: In December 2008, Japanese industrial output fell by almost 10 percent from the previous month, and in April 2009 the country experienced its first trade deficit in nearly 30 years (Japan Statistics Bureau, 2011).

By early 2011, Japan's economy looked as if it was ready to recover, but the earthquake-tsunami-radiation disaster of March 11 slowed industrial production, increased fuel imports and led to a further spike in the value of the yen. This triple disaster contributed to an expected 0.7 percent decline in real GDP growth for 2011, and, according to preliminary estimates, the country's first annual merchandise trade deficit since 1963 (IMF, 2011; "Japan's Trade Balance: Seeing Red," 2012).

**The economic fallout from the Tohoku earthquake may be long lasting.** The Japanese economy is still feeling the effects of earthquake-induced shortages that contributed to an 8 percent drop in exports over the three months following the disaster (Japan Ministry of Finance, 2012). However, manufacturers are beginning to restore capacity in the critical parts and components factories that were damaged in March, as shown by the rebound in Japanese industrial production over those same three months. Of greater concern is the energy situation: Japan relies on nuclear power for roughly 30 percent of its electricity; prior to the earthquake, it was projected to increase this reliance to as much as 50 percent by 2050 (U.S. Energy Information Administration, 2011). This now seems unlikely. Instead, Japan will probably look to other sources of energy, such as coal, liquefied natural gas, and renewable energy, much of which will have to be imported. In the meantime, the combination of electricity shortages due to the Fukushima disaster and sharp appreciation of the yen has been pushing more Japanese manufacturing companies overseas, exacerbating the hollowing out of the Japanese economy.

---

[1] Note, however, that while Japan's GDP growth has lagged since the bursting of the bubble economy, per-capita consumption, life expectancy, health standards, and other indicators of Japanese well-being have improved substantially in the past 20 years (Fingleton, 2012).

Japan's food security policies are also at risk: Plans to raise Japan's food self-sufficiency from 40 percent to 50 percent are now compromised by the contamination of agricultural land in Tohoku and neighboring regions ("Tsunami Risk to Japan's Self-Sufficiency in Rice," 2011; Bosveld, 2011).[2] Finally, a big concern for Japanese policymakers is how to pay for reconstruction after the earthquake, as there is considerable resistance both to taking on new debt and to raising taxes.

**The service sector dominates the economy.** As in the United States, services account for slightly more than three-quarters of Japanese economic activity, followed by the nonfarm goods-producing sector (23 percent) and the agricultural sector (1 percent) in 2008. On the employment front, the service industries provide the most jobs, led by wholesale and retail trade, unspecified services, and health care. Within the goods-producing sector, manufacturing is the largest contributor to GDP at 20 percent, led by transportation equipment, which accounts for 12.7 percent of GDP (Japan Statistics Bureau, 2011).

**Japan's government debt is the highest in the world.** In 2011 Japan's government debt was over 200 percent of GDP, the highest of any country in the world. The Tohoku earthquake means that Japan's debt-to-GDP ratio will almost certainly go higher in 2011, perhaps as high as 230 percent—which is more than twice the ratio in the United States (IMF, 2011). High and rising debt ratios are problematic for most governments because they make it more difficult—and more expensive—to find and keep investors. They are less of a problem for Japan, however, because of high Japanese savings rates. Japan's government debt is denominated in yen and mostly held by Japanese, so that there is little prospect of a Japanese debt sell-off leading to a currency or banking crisis.[3] Further, Japan's weak economy means that the Bank of Japan may be able to purchase much of the debt itself, if necessary, without fear of igniting inflation. Nevertheless, the credit agency Standard & Poor's lowered Japan's "AA–" sovereign credit rating, already the fourth-highest grade, from "stable" to "negative" as a result of the earthquake (Ito and Ujikane, 2011).[4] Although officials passed a bill in November 2011 that will raise revenue through income tax hikes and sales of government assets, much of the cost of earthquake reconstruction is being financed through borrowing (Ma, 2011; Ikeda, Yui, and Fujioka, 2011).

**An aging population and shrinking labor force will constrain future economic growth.** Japan's labor force numbered 66.2 million people in 2009, down 1.7 million (2.6 percent) from its historical high in 1998 (Japan Statistics Bureau, 2011). While there is still some room for expansion if more women and elderly people enter the labor force, declining birth rates mean that the labor force will continue to shrink in the long run unless current restrictive immigration policies are changed. The population is also getting older, which is putting pressure on the public pension system—a situation that will only get worse in the future as retired workers begin to dissave. The combination of an aging population and declining labor force is also leading to significant shortages of health care workers. Finally, a shrinking labor force—and possibly a shrinking capital stock, if dissaving is severe—must eventually reduce Japanese output unless very large gains in productivity can be made. This seems unlikely without sig-

---

[2]  Food self-sufficiency is measured on a calorie supply basis.

[3]  Foreigners held approximately 8.2 percent of Japanese government debt as of December 2011, close to the all-time high of 8.5 percent in the third quarter of 2008 (McLannahan, 2012).

[4]  The credit agencies Standard & Poor's and Fitch both rate Japan's government debt at AA–; Moody's lowered its rating on Japan's debt to AA– in August 2011 (Ito and Anstey, 2011).

nificant reforms, however, because—outside of the showcase export industries—Japan's labor force productivity is relatively low by industrialized country standards.[5] This is particularly true for the service sector, the fastest growing segment of the Japanese economy (Lincoln, 2001).

**Japan's economy is still export-led.** Japanese exports averaged just over 15 percent of GDP over the five years ending in 2009, a smaller percentage than that of other big trading nations such as Germany (44 percent), China (35 percent), and the United Kingdom (28 percent), but more than that of the United States (11 percent) (World Bank, 2011). Japan's relatively small export share is misleading, however, because exports still effectively drive the economy. During the "lost decade" of the 1990s, for example, net exports (the value of exports less imports) were flat and the economy stalled. From 2002 to 2007, exports surged and, if capital spending by exporters is included, net exports accounted for almost half of Japan's total GDP growth. However, in 2009 the weak world economy and strong yen contributed to a 25 percent decline in exports, the largest percentage decrease since 1945. Exports have since rebounded, but concerns about an over-reliance on foreign demand persist (Japan Statistics Bureau, 2011).

**Asian countries dominate Japanese trade.** The list of Japan's top trading partners has been dominated by Asian countries, which collectively accounted for more than 55 percent of total Japanese trade in 2010. Japan's top five partners in terms of their share of the value of total Japanese trade (exports plus imports) in 2010 were China (20.7 percent of total trade), the United States (12.7 percent), South Korea (6.2 percent), Taiwan (5.2 percent), and Australia (4.2 percent). 2010 marked the second year that China was Japan's top trading partner, replacing the United States, which is now second (Japan Statistics Bureau, 2011).

**Automobiles dominate goods exports; services exports are negligible.** In 2010, motor vehicles accounted for 12.4 percent of total exports by value, reflecting the continued dominance of high-value-added manufactured products in Japanese exports (Japan Statistics Bureau, 2011). Despite the importance of services to domestic economic activity, Japan has for many years run deficits in its services trade, with the growth in royalty receipts from the overseas subsidiaries of Japanese companies more than offset by negative balances in transportation services (mostly freight and port services) and tourism (Japan Statistics Bureau, 2011).

**Japanese manufacturing is moving overseas.** More than two-thirds of Japanese manufacturers had overseas production sites in 2009, and overseas production accounted for 18 percent of Japanese manufacturing firms' output in fiscal 2009—a percentage that has been rising rapidly. Japanese FDI is motivated by a number of factors, including the need to cater to local markets, a strong yen, and barriers to trade. In the electronics sector, especially, where Japan is a leader in producing high-value components and parts, FDI is also driven by participation in the production networks that have sprung up throughout East Asia. In fact, there is considerable concern in Japan about the "hollowing out" of domestic manufacturing as more products—and more jobs—are transferred to such places as Thailand and China.[6] There is

---

[5] In 2010, for example, total labor productivity in Japan (measured as GDP per hour worked) was just 67 percent of total labor productivity in the United States. In the same year, Germany's total labor productivity was 91 percent of U.S. total labor productivity and British total labor productivity was 78 percent (OECD, 2012).

[6] Some of this concern should be moderated by the fact that Japan receives sizable earnings from its overseas direct investments, so much so that, for the past several years, Japan's current account surplus has been nearly twice its trade surplus (Japan Statistics Bureau, 2011).

also concern about technology leakage to competitors, especially those located in China, South Korea, and Taiwan (Japan Statistics Bureau, 2011).

**A large percentage of Japanese manufacturers' sales and profits derive from subsidiaries based in Asia.** Cumulatively, the countries with the largest amount of Japanese direct investment as of 2010 were the United States, the Netherlands, China, and Australia. On a flow basis, the top three targets were the United States, Australia, and China. But the real story comes from the sales and operating profits of manufacturing firms. In the first quarter of 2010, almost 40 percent of the sales and 50 percent of the operating profits of Japanese manufacturing firms came from overseas subsidiaries. Of those overseas sales and profits, more than one-third of the sales and more than one-half of the profits came from subsidiaries based in Asia. Nonmanufacturing firms have a much smaller overseas presence (roughly 17 percent of sales and 13 percent of profits) but are even more heavily concentrated in Asia (48 percent of overseas sales and 55 percent of overseas profits) (Japan Statistics Bureau, 2011). Products manufactured by the subsidiaries of Japanese firms are sold all over the world, but the biggest markets for these products include Japan, the United States, the European Union, and increasingly, other Asian countries (METI, 2011).

**Despite highly protected agricultural markets, Japan relies heavily on imported food.** Agriculture represents a tiny proportion of the Japanese economy, accounting for just 1.1 percent of Japan's GDP and just 3.9 percent of its workforce. In 2005, there were approximately 2 million farm households engaged in commercial farming, more than half of which were headed by farmers over 65 years old.[7] Of these farm households, 22.6 percent were full-time farm households, 15.7 percent were part-time farm households with farming income exceeding nonfarming income, and 61.7 percent were part-time farm households with nonfarming income exceeding farming income (Japan Statistics Bureau, 2011). At an average size of three hectares, nearly three-quarters of Japanese farms are well below the minimum efficient size for production (Godo, 2007). All of Japan's major crops are heavily protected by measures that add as much as 778 percent (rice), 379 percent (sugar), 252 percent (wheat), 218 percent (dairy products), and 50 percent (beef) to their world market price. Nevertheless, Japan is one of the world's largest net importers of agricultural products, and it has the lowest food self-sufficiency rate, 39 percent, of any developed country (WTO, 2011).

## The Evolution of Japanese Trade Policy

**Japan was a latecomer to preferential trade.** Prior to 2000, Japanese policymakers were quite critical of preferential arrangements. They believed that FTAs posed a threat to the multilateral world trading system, which has greatly benefited Japan (Kono, 2001). A number of developments in the late 1990s, however, caused them to rethink their position on FTAs.

- The 1997 Asian financial crisis revealed the extent of Japan's dependence on the economic health of its regional trade partners.
- Japanese policymakers, like those in the United States, began to suspect that the Doha Round might not be able to achieve the goals of most interest to Japanese firms—in fact, that it might not be concluded at all.

---

[7]  Commercial farm households are defined as households with cultivated land under management of 0.3 hectares or more, or with annual sales of agricultural products amounting to 500,000 yen or more (Japan Statistics Bureau, 2011).

- They became increasingly nervous about being left out by preferential arrangements involving trading partners: By 2001, Japan and Korea were the only OECD countries that had not entered into a FTA.
- Some Japanese policymakers sought to use FTAs as means to stimulate deregulation and restructuring of their own stagnant economy.
- They saw FTAs as means of furthering liberalization while keeping the most sensitive practices and sectors (such as agriculture) off of the negotiating table.

**Japan has been strategic in its approach to FTAs.** By 2001, when approached by Singapore to form a FTA, Japan was ready to try the experiment. In a policy paper, the Ministry of Foreign Affairs (MoFA) outlined parameters for Japanese involvement in preferential arrangements, stating that Japan would seek to establish FTAs that liberalize investment and encourage broad economic cooperation in addition to reducing barriers to trade (Urata, 2011). MoFA suggested that it is generally in Japan's interest to use economic cooperation to help other countries develop because, if they are successful, they can stimulate growth in the Japanese economy through exports. However, MoFA also argued that partners should be selected strategically, on the basis of certain economic, geographic, political, and "readiness" criteria. Based on these selection criteria, MoFA concluded that South Korea and the countries of Southeast Asia, particularly the ASEAN countries, should be Japan's highest priorities for initiating FTAs (Urata, 2005; MoFA, 2010; Lord, 2010).

**Japan has acted quickly on its strategic embrace of bilateralism and regionalism.** Although Japan has not generally been the instigator of the FTAs it has joined, it has responded quickly to overtures from countries that meet its FTA selection criteria. As shown in Table 2, between 2002 and August 2011, Japan implemented twelve bilateral FTAs, including a regional FTA with ASEAN.[8] Another three FTAs are in the process of being negotiated or concluded. On examination of this list, Japan's pro-Asia strategy is evident: Seven of its twelve bilateral partners—Singapore, Malaysia, Thailand, Indonesia, Brunei, the Philippines, and Vietnam—are members of ASEAN. Japan's desire to avoid being shut out by other countries' FTAs is also clear: Mexico, for example, provides an important entry to the U.S. market through NAFTA, while Chile has established FTAs with countries across Central America and the Pacific. Further, a number of Japan's current and prospective FTA partners are countries that supply mineral resources: Indonesia and the GCC are oil and natural gas producers, Australia is a source for coal and iron ore, and Chile and Peru are important sources for copper ore and other minerals (Park, Urata, and Cheong, 2005).

**Japanese FTAs are more than free trade agreements.** Japanese FTAs—particularly those with Southeast Asian nations—tend to emphasize trade facilitation, technical assistance, and education and training, all of which fit under the umbrella of "economic cooperation."[9] FTA provisions in these policy areas take many forms, including

- investment in partner countries' logistics infrastructures
- technical assistance to improve partner countries' customs procedures

---

[8]  Japan's FTAs are formally named EPAs (economic partnership agreements) because their coverage is comprehensive and going beyond trade liberalization. However, as discussed below, their coverage is not as comprehensive as that of other FTAs, such as those established by the United States.

[9]  For this reason, the Japanese government calls them "economic partnership agreements" rather than FTAs.

**Table 2**
**Japanese Free Trade Agreements by Partner**

| Partner | FTA Name | Date Signed (PM) | Date Ratified by Diet (PM) | Date in Effect |
|---|---|---|---|---|
| Negotiations concluded or in progress | | | | |
| Singapore | JSEPA | January 2002 (Koizumi) | n.a. | November 2002 |
| Mexico | JUMSEPA[a] | September 2004 (Koizumi) | November 2004 (Koizumi) | March 2005 |
| Malaysia | JMEPA | December 2005 Koizumi) | July 2006 (Koizumi) | July 2006 |
| Philippines | JPEPA | September 2006 (Koizumi) | December 2006 (Abe) | December 2008 |
| Chile | JCEPA | March 2007 (Abe) | June 2007 (Abe) | September 2007 |
| Thailand | JTEPA | April 2007 (Abe) | October 2007 (Fukuda) | November 2007 |
| Indonesia | JIEPA | August 2007 (Abe) | June 2008 (Fukuda) | July 2008 |
| Brunei | JBEPA | June 2007 (Abe) | n.a. | July 2008 |
| ASEAN[b] | AJCEP | April 2008 (Fukuda) | June 2008 (Fukuda) | December 2008 |
| Switzerland | JSFTEPA[c] | February 2009 (Aso) | June 2009 (Aso) | September 2009 |
| Vietnam | Japan-Vietnam EPA | December 2008 (Aso) | June 2009 (Aso) | October 2009 |
| India | Japan-India EPA | February 2011 (Kan) | June 2011 (Kan) | August 2011 |
| Peru | Japan-Peru EPA | May 2011 (Kan) | June 2011 (Kan) | TBD 2012 |
| GCC[d] | Japan-GCC EPA | Negotiations in progress (since 2006) | | |
| Australia | Japan-Australia EPA | Negotiations in progress (since 2007) | | |
| Negotiations suspended | | | | |
| Korea | Japan-Korea EPA | Negotiations began 2003; suspended 2004 | | |

SOURCE: MoFA, 2012.

[a] Agreement between Japan and the United Mexican States for the Strengthening of the Economic Partnership.

[b] Association of Southeast Asian Nations.

[c] Japan-Switzerland Free Trade and Economic Partnership Agreement.

[d] Gulf Cooperation Council.

NOTE: n.a. = not applicable.

- technical assistance to small and medium-sized enterprises (SMEs) in partner countries
- facilitation of educational and professional exchanges.

Specific examples from the FTA with Singapore include the cross-recognition of electrical safety standards, cross-recognition of undergraduate college credits, and cooperation between the two countries' stock exchanges. FTAs with the Philippines and Indonesia both include provisions that expand the number of visas available for nurses coming to Japan (Kimura and Kuno, 2007; Lord, 2010).

**Japanese FTAs are not as comprehensive as U.S. FTAs.** Japanese FTAs are not as comprehensive as U.S. FTAs in their coverage of WTO-plus issues.[10] With the exception of investment, Japan has generally taken a positive-list approach to liberalization, opening only selected sectors. No additional environmental safeguards or labor standards protections are included in Japanese FTAs. Further, upon closer examination, many of the "cooperation" provisions in Japanese FTAs are not as impressive as they may first appear. For example, the number of nurses allowed into Japan under the Japan-Philippines FTA is restricted to no more than 1,000 over two years—and the program is restricted to caregivers who can pass a rigorous language exam. As of March 2011, only one Filipina nurse out of 257 participants had successfully passed the exam.

**Agriculture is conspicuously missing from Japanese FTAs.** But the defining characteristic of Japan's FTAs—indeed, of Japan's trade policy in general—is the complete omission of agricultural goods from liberalization. In Japan's FTA with Singapore, for example, just 486 out of 2,227 agricultural product categories included in the tariff classification system were selected for liberalization—and all of these were either already essentially duty-free or already scheduled to be cut as a result of prior WTO agreements. When measured by tariff line code, just 76 percent of tariff lines were liberalized in JSEPA, 86 percent in Japan's FTA with Mexico, and 89 percent in its FTA with Malaysia—low percentages by the standards of U.S. FTAs—and almost entirely due to continued high tariffs on agricultural imports. In fact, the Japan-Mexico FTA was nearly scuttled due to Japanese protection of domestic pork. Japan and Peru struggled to reach agreement over fish, and the proposed Japan-Australia FTA is still in limbo due to conflicts over dairy products and sugar (Park, Urata, and Cheong, 2005).

---

[10] WTO-plus generally refers to treatment of trade issues or topics that exceed existing WTO requirements.

# CHAPTER SEVEN

# The Japanese Political Environment

## Japanese Trade Politics—Actors and Issues

**The Democratic Party of Japan (DPJ) won the 2009 election with a platform promising change.** The DPJ party platform of August 2009 had five main elements: eliminate government waste; provide incentives for child-rearing and education; reform pension and medical care systems; provide more local political autonomy; and stimulate the economy and employment. Specific pledges included consolidating and scaling down the U.S. military air base in Okinawa and liberalizing trade and investment by pursuing an FTA with the United States.

**There have been three DPJ prime ministers since the August 2009 election, none of whom has been seen as a strong leader on trade.** Prime Minister Hatoyama was forced to resign in June 2010 due to his inability to deliver on most of the DPJ's pledges, in particular the pledge to close down the Okinawa military base. Hatoyama was succeeded by his finance minister, Naoto Kan, who was forced to step down in August 2011 in large part because of his perceived ineffectiveness in dealing with the Tohoku earthquake. The current prime minister, Yoshihiko Noda, was finance minister under Kan. His declared priorities include rebuilding after the earthquake, weakening the surging yen, reducing the government debt and unifying his fractious party. Noda had made cautiously supportive statements about joining the TPP in the past, but given the opposition to agricultural reform within his own party, it was not clear prior to his November 7 announcement which way he would go.

**Agricultural reform is a "wedge" issue that cuts across party lines for Japanese legislators.** Agricultural reform in Japan is a deeply divisive issue. Due in part to the disproportionate strength of the rural vote in Japan, agricultural groups such as the Central Union of Agricultural Cooperatives (Nokyo) still hold considerable sway over trade policy. They greatly fear the potential loss of jobs and livelihoods that may result if agricultural markets are opened up to more productive foreign producers. A November 2009 legislative survey revealed that roughly half of LDP legislators and nearly one-fourth of DPJ legislators opposed the idea of a U.S.-Japan FTA because of its potential negative impact on Japanese farmers. Of those legislators that supported the FTA, almost one-third of Liberal Democratic Party (LDP) members and nearly half of DPJ members preferred to exclude some agricultural products from such an agreement (Krauss and Naoi, 2011). Nonetheless, there is some reason to believe that a change in agricultural policy is possible. The DPJ came to power promoting a new agricultural policy that would provide direct subsidies to farmers in return for a more open market. And interviews with both LDP and DPJ legislators indicate that support for policies that would enable more productive agriculture through land consolidation also spans party lines.

**Japanese consumers are mixed on the opening of domestic agricultural markets.** According to a survey conducted by the Japanese Cabinet Office, the percentage of Japanese consumers who prefer higher-priced domestic agricultural products to lower-priced imports climbed from approximately 30 percent in 1987 to approximately 50 percent in 2008. In a separate survey conducted in February 2009, more than 55 percent of the consumers surveyed stated that, in order to protect Japanese agriculture, Japan "should not accept import liberalization of agricultural products" (Naoi and Kume, 2010). The most common reasons for opposing agricultural import liberalization were food security—the desire to ensure adequate domestic food sources in case of disturbances to external food supplies—and food safety. Contributing factors include concerns over foreign suspensions and embargoes of food exports, and a number of scandals involving tainted imported food. The Ministry of Agriculture, Fishery and Forestry (MAFF) and Nokyo have played upon these concerns, mounting an extensive public relations campaign on behalf of agricultural import protection (Naoi and Kume, 2010).

**Japanese business groups see domestic agricultural reform as both necessary and desirable.** Japanese business leaders represented by the Japan Business Federation (Keidanren) are desirous of more economic integration in the Asia-Pacific region to enable them to create seamless transnational supply chains and production networks. These businesses see agricultural reform as necessary for participation in the multilateral, regional, and bilateral trade agreements that will enable this integration, which they view as key to Japan's continued economic growth and well-being. To Japanese business groups, therefore, the need to reform Japan's agricultural sector is evident. In their view, the rapidly shrinking Japanese farm population and low average productivity of Japanese farms is preventing Japan from achieving food security, while domestic food safety is now being threatened by the Fukushima radiation leak. Instead of protecting farmers from import competition, Keidanren argues that Japan would be better served by

- prohibiting export restrictions in food exporting countries
- continuing to supplement the domestic food supply with imports
- consolidating and mechanizing Japanese agriculture so that it becomes more efficient
- harmonizing international safety standards for imported foods
- improving the system for identifying and reporting food safety incidents.

**Japanese political leaders worry about rising Chinese influence in the region.** Like their U.S. counterparts, Japanese political leaders are worried about the proliferation of Chinese FTAs in the Asia-Pacific region—as well as China's assertiveness in a number of noneconomic areas, including its territorial claims and support for rogue regimes, such as North Korea. Japan is particularly worried that an economically dominant China will use trade policy tools to retaliate against countries with which it has disagreements. This has happened before: In September 2010, for example, China banned exports of rare earth minerals to Japan in response to a diplomatic incident involving the Japanese arrest of a Chinese fishing boat captain (Gordon, 2011).

# CHAPTER EIGHT

# Assessing Trade Policy Options

## The Four Options

Prior to Prime Minister Noda's decision, the United States and Japan had four main options for their trade policies toward each other: (1) working together to revive the multilateral Doha Round of the WTO, (2) signing a bilateral FTA, (3) participating in the TPP, and (4) continuing to pursue independent trade strategies. These options were not all mutually exclusive; in fact, it is likely that both countries will continue to pursue some sort of conclusion to the Doha Round while simultaneously engaging in negotiations for the TPP. However, limited time and resources will likely require them to focus their negotiating attention on the TPP. In this chapter, we examine those decisions in light of the policy environments discussed above.

### Option 1. Joint U.S.-Japan Efforts to Revitalize the Doha Round ("Revive Doha")

U.S. and Japanese policymakers together decide that the failure of the Doha Round is a major threat to the rules-based international trading system. To get the round going again, both countries agree to make concessions to the developing world, with the United States agreeing to cut some of its agricultural subsidies and Japan agreeing to open some of its agricultural markets. The new round contains provisions that promote both trade and investment.

### Option 2. A U.S.-Japan FTA ("Bilateral FTA")

The United States and Japan establish a U.S.-Japan bilateral FTA. U.S. exporters gain access to some previously closed Japanese markets, including some agriculture and services markets, and Japanese exporters and investors gain greater protection against U.S. antidumping measures as well as a greater assurance that they will not be discriminated against by future U.S. FTAs, particularly KORUS. The bilateral pact contains provisions that promote both trade and investment.

### Option 3. U.S.-Japan Cooperation Through the TPP ("Trans-Pacific Partnership")

Japan decides to join the United States, Singapore, Brunei, New Zealand, Chile, Australia, Peru, Vietnam, and Malaysia in negotiating the TPP. In return for greater access to TPP-member markets and the opportunity to participate in the development of standardized rules and systems for governing international trade and investment in the Asia-Pacific region, Japan is required to liberalize most if not all of its agricultural goods markets. The United States, too, agrees to open most of its most sensitive goods markets (e.g., sugar, dairy products) as part of the TPP negotiations.

**Option 4. Continuation of Current Policies ("Status Quo")**

U.S. trade policymakers concentrate on promoting comprehensive trade and investment liberalization through the TPP, and seek to expand TPP membership to like-minded countries. Japan decides to delay joining the TPP, focusing instead on partners and pacts that do not require liberalization of its agricultural sector. Neither country makes any serious effort to revive the Doha Round.

## Assessment

According to our analysis, the preferred trade policy option for each country should be the one that is best able to meet five broad objectives identified through readings and interviews:

1. Strengthen the country's international reputation.
2. Stimulate the domestic economy in the short run.
3. Promote long-run economic growth.
4. Achieve broad political acceptability at home.
5. Allow implementation notwithstanding (or by overcoming) domestic and international political and economic constraints.

We do not mean to suggest that these five objectives will be evenly weighted or that the United States and Japan will assign the same weights and priorities to each objective. And we recognize that both the United States and Japan are likely to value short- and long-term economic growth over concerns about their international reputations. Furthermore, a successful trade policy will always depend on whether or not the negotiated agreement can gain the needed approval from the legislative body (this idea is captured in objective number four above). Success in trade agreements also depends on the amount of time, energy, and political capital the executive branch (or cabinet in the case of Japan) is willing to expend on its behalf, not only on the front end negotiating the deal but also on the back end selling the deal to the legislature and other interested parties. This is the idea behind objective number five above.

### Assessment of Option 1: Revive Doha

**Objective 1: Strengthen international reputation.** Many countries blame the United States for the breakdown of the Doha Round trade talks in Geneva in 2008. The United States would likely be praised for its leadership should U.S. policymakers restart the talks with an offer to reduce or eliminate U.S. agricultural subsidies—one of the key demands of developing-country participants in the talks. Japan has a reputation for political paralysis when it comes to undertaking difficult internal economic reforms, particularly in the area of agriculture. By agreeing to open its agricultural markets to help bring Doha to a successful conclusion, Japan would greatly strengthen its international reputation.

**Objective 2: Stimulate the domestic economy in the short run.** According to one study, the package proposed at the July 2008 meeting would have increased annual U.S. and Japanese merchandise goods exports by $6 billion and $7 billion, respectively—representing gains of just 0.4 and 0.9 percent over 2007 levels for each country (Adler et al., 2009). This suggests that, for the United States and Japan, the immediate stimulative effects of a Doha agreement would be fairly small—even in the event that all of its provisions were put into effect immediately, which is highly unlikely.

**Objective 3: Promote long-run economic growth.** The economic impact of concluding the Doha Round would be significantly greater in the long run than in the short run. One reason is that liberalization measures are typically introduced in phases, so that implementation is gradual. More important, domestic firms and markets will continue to adjust over time to the increased competition that will result from Doha. Long-term adjustments may include the development of new products and processes; the globalization of supply chains; the development of scale economies in international shipping, distribution, and marketing; and measures to improve labor productivity—including more education for the workforce. In sum, there is a strong empirical link between trade openness, productivity, and economic growth.

**Objective 4: Achieve broad political acceptability at home.** The key to reviving Doha appears to be the elimination of U.S. agricultural subsidies combined with improved access to nonagricultural markets in large emerging countries. In the United States, politically powerful agricultural interests strongly oppose the elimination of subsidies but might be amenable to an agreement if Japan (or some other large potential market) made offsetting agricultural concessions. U.S. manufacturers and service providers, however, would completely oppose any deal that failed to significantly reduce barriers to access in Brazil, China, and India. Politically speaking, no U.S. government can afford to be seen as tolerating perceived "free riders" in the multilateral world trading system.

In Japan, the large concessions on agriculture that would be required to revive Doha would meet with tremendous political resistance. Japanese supporters of trade liberalization, including influential business groups, would prefer to focus their efforts on FTAs, because FTAs have the potential to offer them more in such priority areas as foreign direct investment, intellectual property rights, and government procurement. Further, it may be easier for them to persuade Japanese policymakers to participate in FTAs: first, because FTAs can have more flexibility than the WTO with respect to "sensitive products," and second, because the adverse impact on Japanese agriculture may be smaller because fewer countries are involved.

**Objective 5: Be relatively easy to implement.** Since the collapse of talks in July 2008, WTO member countries have held a series of meetings to try and revive the Doha Round— but there have been no breakthroughs, and the likelihood of one appears to be diminishing. Prospects for a joint U.S.-Japanese effort to revive Doha in 2012 are particularly gloomy: U.S. policymakers will be reluctant to make any moves on trade prior to the presidential elections in November; in Japan, the DPJ is still split on the issue of agricultural reform and liberalization. Presidential elections in India and a scheduled change of leadership in China will further complicate any attempt to reach agreement on a multilateral Doha package next year. The year 2013 looks more promising for U.S. action because the U.S. president's attention will again be free to turn toward trade. However, 2013 is a general election year in Japan, so prospects then for Japanese action on Doha are slim.

### Assessment of Option 2: A U.S.-Japan Bilateral FTA

**Objective 1: Strengthen international reputation.** A bilateral FTA with Japan would likely have strengthened U.S.-Japanese political and security cooperation, in addition to offering some economic benefits. It would not, however, have served the purpose of creating a platform for economic integration in the region, and so would not have raised the U.S. profile in the region by very much. With respect to Japan, Japanese policymakers as recently as 2009 viewed a bilateral trade pact with the United States as a possible way for Japan to solidify its security relationship with the United States and preclude any possibility of trade isolation. At the same time, they feared that a bilateral pact could lead to a recurrence of the friction that characterized U.S.-Japan trade relations in the 1980s. On net, it is not clear whether a U.S.-Japan FTA would have improved U.S.-Japan relations. It also is not clear what such a pact would have meant for Japan's international reputation, as Japan has long had close political and economic ties to the United States.

**Objective 2: Stimulate the domestic economy in the short run.** We found no recent studies that estimate the potential economic impact of a U.S.-Japan bilateral FTA. But because Japan and the United States represent roughly 6 and 16 percent of each other's total merchandise trade, respectively, the impact on merchandise trade would likely be less than for a WTO agreement, which would cover over 95 percent of trade for both countries. On the other hand, a U.S.-Japan FTA would likely be more comprehensive than Doha, so that the impact in areas such as services, investment, and nontariff barriers would be greater. As with Doha, any tariff reductions or other liberalization measures would almost certainly be introduced in phases so as to allow domestic industries and workers time to adjust. In the short term, therefore, the economic impact of such an agreement would likely be small.

**Objective 3: Promote long-run economic growth.** In the long term, greater competition resulting from market opening would likely be particularly important for the restructuring of the Japanese economy.

**Objective 4: Achieve broad political acceptability at home.** In Japan, there is strong opposition from the powerful agricultural lobby to any trade pact that threatens to reduce or eliminate domestic agricultural protections. In the United States, FTAs that do not promise to provide significant market opportunities for agricultural exporters are typically opposed— or at least not supported—by the powerful U.S. agricultural lobby. Further, because of the legacy of mistrust that has carried over from the trade disputes of the 1980s, many Japanese and American producers in nonagricultural sectors tend to be cautious or even skeptical about the gains that can be achieved in a bilateral U.S.-Japan setting. These factors were all present in 2009, when the DPJ party platform called for the formation of a U.S.-Japan FTA. When pressure from Japanese farmers forced the DPJ to promise not to reduce domestic agricultural protection, U.S. farmers lost interest in the deal. No other strong supporters emerged. By 2011, the opportunity for a bilateral FTA had passed.

**Objective 5: Be relatively easy to implement.** Any possible bilateral U.S.-Japan FTA has been subsumed into the TPP. For the foreseeable future, this option is off the table.

### Assessment of Option 3: Trans-Pacific Partnership

**Objective 1: Strengthen international reputation.** By joining the TPP negotiations, the United States has signaled its commitment to the Asia-Pacific reegion and to Asia-Pacific markets. Ultimately, the United States sees the TPP as a means to ensure that it retains its economic and political leadership in Asia and does not get shut out by the many existing and proposed FTAs between and among Asian countries and the rest of the world. Specifically, the United States hopes that the TPP will help it to counterbalance Chinese economic and political influence in the region. Japanese participation is key to achieving that end.

The decision to participate in the TPP has signaled Japan's own commitment to Asia-Pacific integration and its desire to retain economic leadership within the region. It also expresses Japan's willingness to ally itself with the United States in a regional bloc that—for the time being—excludes China. Perhaps most important, Japan's participation in the TPP indicates a readiness to open itself up to the rest of the world, to give as well as to take in equal partnership with other trading nations.

**Objective 2: Stimulate the domestic economy in the short run.** Because details of the TPP negotiations have not yet been released, it is not possible to estimate what the likely economic impact of the pact will be for the United States. However, the decision to participate in itself may have benefited the United States by signaling U.S. interest in further economic liberalization and regional integration, both of which make the United States an attractive place to invest. For Japan, the signaling effect of joining the TPP could be very important, helping to slow or perhaps even reverse the exodus of Japanese companies that are in search of more dynamic production locations overseas. This hollowing out phenomenon has been magnified by uncertainties introduced by the Tohoku earthquake. By reassuring Japanese companies that their domestic market will in future offer greater opportunities for growth, some companies that are now on the fence about keeping their production operations in Japan may be persuaded to remain. Some foreign companies may also be persuaded to invest in Japan.

**Objective 3: Promote long-run economic growth.** If the TPP turns out to be as comprehensive as its supporters claim it will, it has the potential to have a significant long-term impact on both the U.S. and Japanese economies. The long-term effect on the Japanese economy will likely be larger, because the Japanese economy is more protected—and therefore less productive. Specifically, the TPP will have many of the same effects as described above for Doha and for the U.S.-Japan FTA. Because, with the inclusion of Japan, it will consist of ten partner countries, it should have a greater economic impact on both Japan and the United States than would the bilateral U.S.-Japan FTA. The relative impact of the TPP versus Doha is not as clear, because Doha covers more countries while the TPP (presumably) is more comprehensive.

**Objective 4: Achieve broad political acceptability at home.** There has been no real test yet of U.S. policymakers' willingness to make concessions in such sensitive areas as cotton, sugar, textiles, and automobiles, partly because the details of the TPP negotiations are still a closely guarded secret. In addition, through mid-October 2011, advocates on both sides of the liberalization debate were taken up with the fight over the Colombia, Korea, and Panama FTAs. Now that this fight is over, their attention is turning to the TPP. Because Japanese and U.S. companies compete in so many areas, U.S. opponents of liberalization are likely to push much harder against the TPP now that Japan is in it. Consequently, U.S. policymakers have been somewhat ambivalent about Japan's participation.

Prime Minister Noda, together with the Ministry of Economy, Trade and Industry and the Ministry of Foreign Affairs, supported participation in the TPP. The Ministry of Agriculture, Forestry and Fisheries was strongly opposed. The Ministry of Finance appeared most concerned about the possible implications of the TPP for the government budget, which are ambiguous. Outside the government, a public relations battle is raging. It has been dominated by the anti-TPP forces, which have greatly benefited from the deep pockets of the Japanese agricultural cooperatives. Pro-TPP business groups, such as Keidanren, have been much less visible in their support of the pact, but they appear to be ratcheting up their efforts. As more details of the negotiations emerge, this struggle will likely intensify.

**Objective 5: Be relatively easy to implement.** The November 11–13, 2011, APEC summit in Honolulu provided an important target deadline for Japan: TPP advocates had argued that if the government delayed its decision past that point, Japan might not be able to influence the rules or agenda for the group. The APEC meeting's Honolulu location may also have been important to the United States, giving President Obama the opportunity to play up the TPP and the U.S. position as a Pacific nation. In the future, TPP members are targeting July 2012 for completion of a broad outline of the pact. Whether this is achievable given the political realities in the United States and other member countries remains to be seen.

## Assessment of Option 4: Status Quo

**Objective 1: Strengthen international reputation.** If the United States and Japan both effectively abandon Doha, both countries will be perceived as lacking leadership, although the collapse will probably be blamed more on the United States than on Japan. If Japan had decided not to participate in the TPP, many countries, including the United States, could have interpreted the decision as reflective of a political problem that would likely cause Japan to become progressively more isolated as other countries move forward with comprehensive trade pacts. So, for example, the same obstacles that would have prevented Japan from committing to the TPP would also have meant that Japan would not get very far with a China-Japan-Korea FTA or a FTA with the European Union. The United States would also have lost if Japan had not joined the TPP, because the decision would have set back U.S. plans for a Free Trade Area of the Asia Pacific.

**Objective 2: Stimulate the domestic economy in the short run.** Japan's existing FTA strategy might well have helped it to secure access to raw material resources and ensure the security and stability of its global supply chains. It would not, however, have helped Japan to expand its export markets very much, so it would have been unlikely to provide an immediate economic stimulus. Similarly, the TPP without Japan would not do much to expand U.S. exports both because it covers such a small percentage of U.S. trade and because many of its members are already in FTAs with the United States.

**Objective 3: Promote long-run economic growth.** Expansion of trade, particularly in the Asia-Pacific, is a key component of the U.S. strategy to retain high levels of economic growth. To ensure U.S. economic growth through trade—and to achieve U.S. goals for Asia-Pacific economic integration—the United States needs Japan to join the TPP. For Japan, however, the key to long-term economic vitality is economic restructuring and reform. Restructuring is necessary because large parts of the Japanese economy, including much of the service sector as well as the agricultural sector, have seen little growth in productivity since at least the "lost decade" of the 1990s. Without the TPP or some other strong stimulus to reform, Japan will likely not be able to attract much foreign investment. More important, it may continue to lose Japanese companies to overseas production locations, thereby continuing the economic stagnation that has persisted for almost twenty years.

**Objective 4: Achieve broad political acceptability at home.** Maintaining the status quo might well have been the easiest option for both countries, politically. In the United States, anti-trade activists are gearing up for their assault on the TPP, and U.S. policymakers might have found it easier to promote the pact if Japan was not a participant. In Japan, the agriculture lobby is very strong, and the Japanese public is very worried about food security and safety. Japanese consumers also appear to be quite sympathetic to the concerns of farmers. It will take a concerted, well-thought-out public relations campaign by pro-trade lobby groups to counteract the negative portrayal of the TPP that has already been presented by the agricultural lobby. In both countries, it is probably already too late to save the Doha Round, as Japan has little leverage and the United States wants more concessions from the large emerging market countries.

**Objective 5: Be relatively easy to implement.** Maintaining the status quo would also have been quite practical—the United States and Japan could proceed ahead with their bilateral and regional trade arrangements, none of which require completion of Doha to succeed. The United States and its TPP partners would probably find it easier to meet their July 2012 deadline without Japan.

**Table 3**
**Summary Assessment of Options**

| | United States | Japan |
|---|---|---|
| **Option 1: Revive Doha** | | |
| 1. International reputation | Restores reputation as world leader concerned with world welfare | Helps eliminate reputation for political paralysis |
| 2. Short-run stimulation | Small immediate economic stimulus from expanded exports and investment | Small immediate economic stimulus from expanded exports and investment |
| 3. Long-run economic growth | Expanded exports and investment help boost long-run economic growth | Expanded exports, imports, and investment boost growth and spur competitive restructuring |
| 4. Political acceptability | Strong opposition from the agriculture sector is not balanced by strong support from other sectors | Strong opposition from the agriculture sector not balanced by strong support from other sectors |
| 5. Practicality | Difficult to implement because it requires cooperation from European Union, China, Brazil, and India | Difficult to implement because it requires cooperation from European Union, China, Brazil, and India |
| **Option 2: Bilateral FTA** | | |
| 1. International reputation | Somewhat raises U.S. profile in the Asia-Pacific region | Confirms Japan's close ties to the United States |
| 2. Short-run stimulation | Small immediate economic stimulus from expanded exports and investment | Small immediate economic stimulus from expanded exports and investment |
| 3. Long-run economic growth | Greater economic integration with Japan helps boost long-run economic growth | Greater economic integration with the United States spurs competitive restructuring and boosts growth |
| 4. Political acceptability | U.S. agricultural producers require opening of Japanese markets; nonagricultural producers are skeptical | Strong opposition from agricultural producers; nonagricultural producers insufficiently supportive |
| 5. Practicality | Superseded by TPP | Superseded by TPP |
| **Option 3: Trans-Pacific Partnership** | | |
| 1. International reputation | Raises profile in Asia-Pacific region | Raises profile in Asia-Pacific region |
| 2. Short-run stimulation | Small immediate economic stimulus from expanded exports and investment | Small immediate economic stimulus from expanded exports and investment |
| 3. Long-run economic growth | Greater regional economic integration helps boost long-run economic growth | Greater regional economic integration spurs competitive restructuring and helps boost growth |
| 4. Political acceptability | No real test yet. Japanese participation will likely increase domestic opposition, but may also increase domestic support | Very strong opposition from agricultural sector; support from nonagricultural producers appears to be growing |
| 5. Practicality | July 2012 deadline for completion of an outline may be optimistic | July 2012 deadline for completion of an outline may be optimistic—will Japan ask for more time? |

**Table 3—Continued**

|  | United States | Japan |
|---|---|---|
| **Option 4: Status Quo** | | |
| 1. International reputation | Reputation declines due to failure of Doha Round and inability to expand TPP | Reputation declines due to perception of domestic political paralysis |
| 2. Short-run stimulation | Primary trade stimulus derives from recently negotiated FTAs, such as KORUS | Primary trade stimulus derives from recently negotiated FTAs, such as Japan-India |
| 3. Long-run economic growth | Economic growth linked to growth of Asia-Pacific region; growth prospects diminished if Japan is not in TPP | Lack of reform and slower economic integration implies growing gap between Japan and Asian neighbors |
| 4. Political acceptability | Politically acceptable | Politically acceptable |
| 5. Practicality | Practical | Practical |

# CHAPTER NINE

# Conclusion

In this paper we have examined four trade policy options that were available to the United States and Japan as of the beginning of November 2011: working together to restart the multilateral Doha Round of the WTO, signing a bilateral FTA, participating in the TPP, and continuing with their own independent trade strategies. After examining the economic and political environments in which U.S. and Japanese policymakers operate, and assessing each option based on its ability to achieve broad policy objectives, we conclude that Japan's decision to join the TPP negotiations was the right one—and that U.S. policymakers should welcome Japanese participation in the TPP. Our reasoning follows.

First, participation in the TPP will provide Japan with an opportunity to strengthen its ties to the United States without risking a repeat of the bilateral trade friction that was so prominent during the 1980s. The TPP will situate Japan firmly within the community of Asia-Pacific nations that are among its major trade and investment partners and give it greater economic and political leverage over its largest trading partner, China. From the U.S. perspective, Japan's participation in the TPP is key to ensuring that trade in Asia, the fastest growing region in the world, will be grounded on the principles of free and open trade.

Second, on the economic front, it is unclear what the short-run impact of joining the TPP will mean for the United States or Japan because we do not yet know the exact nature of the concessions that will be required or the timetable for their implementation. To the extent that the TPP is a comprehensive FTA that incorporates areas ranging from food safety to financial services, it will likely have a greater impact than Doha, since the Doha Round's coverage of products and activities is fairly limited. On the other hand, if the Doha Round is ever completed, it will involve many more countries and so a much larger percentage of U.S. and Japanese trade. With respect to the timetable, given the very long phase-in periods that prevail in many current U.S. and Japanese FTAs—and the lack of forward progress on the Doha Round—it seems unlikely that the economic boost from TPP-based liberalization will take longer to achieve than it would under a bilateral FTA or from the conclusion of Doha. In fact, both countries may already be benefiting from their participation in the TPP insofar as the TPP has caused global business to see them as more attractive destinations for investment.

Third, the long-run economic impact of the TPP promises to be significant if participants adhere to its goal of bringing most import tariffs down to zero and eliminating most nontariff barriers to trade. Japan, in particular, should see increases in labor productivity as domestic agriculture and service firms are forced to respond to foreign competition. Both countries should benefit from the creation of a "seamless business environment" across the Pacific, again with Japan probably benefiting the most because, due to its declining population, Japan relies more on foreign demand to drive its economic growth.

Fourth, the political risks associated with significant trade agreements are often high, but a confluence of factors may help to push the TPP through. In Japan, the Tohoku earthquake has magnified a sense of urgency among many political and business leaders, opening the door to bold decisions, such as joining the TPP. The recent signing of the KORUS trade pact and various conflicts with China also helped create an atmosphere conducive to joining. In both the United States and Japan, deep economic recession and the paralysis of the Doha Round have encouraged political leaders to look to FTAs to stimulate exports and thereby generate jobs and economic growth.

Finally, the timing of the TPP so far has turned out to be right: The Honolulu APEC meeting provided a big boost, perhaps influencing the timing of Japan's decision to join. The U.S. presidential election is not yet in full swing and, until quite recently, U.S. opponents of liberalization were focused on killing or stalling the three Bush FTAs. This has allowed U.S. TPP negotiators to operate out of the media spotlight. What will happen when it turns back on remains to be seen.

# Bibliography

Adler, Matthew, Claire Brunel, Gary Clyde Hufbauer, and Jeffrey J. Schott, "What's on the Table? The Doha Round as of August 2009," Peterson Institute for International Economics Working Paper Series, WP 09-6, August 2009. As of November 14, 2011:
http://www.piie.com/publications/wp/wp09-6.pdf

Associated Press, "Regional Free Trade Pact to Allow Exclusions Under Existing Accords," April 1, 2011. As of November 14, 2011:
http://www.breitbart.com/article.php?id=D9MAOSFO1&show_article=1

Barefoot, Kevin B., and Raymond J. Mataloni, Jr., "U.S. Multinational Companies Operations in the United States and Abroad in 2008," *Survey of Current Business,* August 2010, pp. 205–229.

Bergsten, C. Fred, "Toward a Free Trade Area of the Asia Pacific," Peterson Institute for International Economics Policy Brief No. 07-2, February 2007.

———, "U.S. Trade Policy and the Doha Round: An Alternative View," VoxEU.org, 17 May 2011.

Bosveld, Nicole, "Japan's Short-Term Food Crisis Overshadows More Prolonged Emerging Challenge," Future Directions International Strategic Analysis Paper, March 25, 2011. As of January 18, 2012:
http://www.futuredirections.org.au/files/1301389826-FDI%20Strategic%20Analysis%20Paper%2025%20March%202011.pdf

Capling, Ann, "The Trans-Pacific Partnership," *East Asia Forum,* November 23, 2009. As of November 14, 2011:
http://www.eastasiaforum.org/2009/11/23/the-trans-pacific-partnership/

Chase, Kerry A., *Trading Blocs: States, Firms, and Regions in the World Economy,* Ann Arbor, Mich.: University of Michigan Press, 2009.

Cowhey, Peter, "Crafting Trade Strategy in the Great Recession—the Obama Administration and the Change in Political Economy of the United States," University of California, San Diego political science working paper, April 2010.

Destler, I. M., *American Trade Politics,* Fourth Edition, Washington, D.C.: Institute for International Economics, 2005.

Elliott, Larry, "U.S., Europe Risk Double Dip Recession, Warns IMF," *The Guardian,* September 20, 2011. As of November 14, 2011:
http://www.guardian.co.uk/business/2011/sep/20/us-europe-double-dip-recession-imf/print

Elwell, Craig K., "Dumping of Exports and Antidumping Duties: Implications for the U.S. Economy," CRS Report for Congress, No. RL31468, Congressional Research Service, November 2004.

Fingleton, Eamonn, "The Myth of Japan's Failure," *New York Times,* January 8, 2012.

Fergusson, Ian F., and Bruce Vaughn, "The Trans-Pacific Partnership Agreement," CRS Report for Congress, Report No. R40502, Congressional Research Service, June 25, 2010.

Gallagher, Kevin P., "Introduction: International Trade and the Environment," in Kevin P. Gallagher, ed., *Handbook on Trade and the Environment,* Cheltenham, UK: Edward Elgar Publishing, Ltd., 2008, pp. 1–18.

Gantz, David A., "Labor Rights and Environmental Protection Under NAFTA and Other Free Trade Agreements," *Arizona Legal Studies*, Discussion Paper No. 11-13, March 2011.

Garibian, Pablo, and Rachelle Younglai, "Canada, Mexico Ask to Join Pan-Pacific Trade Talks," *Reuters*, November 13, 2011.

Godo, Yoshihisa, "The Puzzle of Small Farming in Japan," Australian National University, Asia Pacific Economic Paper No. 365, 2007. As of January 18, 2012:
http://www.crawford.anu.edu.au/pdf/pep/apep-365.pdf

Gordon, Bernard K., "The Trans-Pacific Partnership and the Rise of China," *Foreign Affairs*, November 7, 2011. As of November 14, 2011:
http://www.foreignaffairs.com/articles/136647/bernard-k-gordon/
the-trans-pacific-partnership-and-the-rise-of-china

Griswold, Daniel, "Unions, Protectionism, and U.S. Competitiveness, *Cato Journal*, Vol. 30, No. 1, Winter 2010.

Harris, Jonathan M., "Trade and the Environment," Tufts University Global Development and Environment Institute Teaching Module, 2004. As of February 1, 2012:
http://www.ase.tufts.edu/gdae/education_materials/modules/Trade_and_the_Environment.pdf

Higley, John, and Michael Sutton, "Progress Report on the North American Free Trade Agreement and Its Implications for U.S. Trade Policy," University of Adelaide Centre for International Studies Working Paper No. 92/2, July 1992.

Hipple, Steven F., "Self-Employment in the United States," *BLS Monthly Labor Review*, September 2010, pp. 17–32.

Horn, Henrik, Petros C. Mavroidis, and Andre Sapir, "Beyond the WTO? An Anatomy of EU and U.S. Preferential Trade Agreements," *Bruegel Blueprint Series*, Vol. VII, 2009.

Hufbauer, Gary Clyde, and Jeffrey J. Schott, *NAFTA Revisited: Achievements and Challenges*, Washington, D.C.: Peterson Institute for International Economics, 2005.

Hufbauer, Gary Clyde, Jeffrey J. Schott and Woan Foong Wong, "Figuring out the Doha Round," *Policy Analyses in International Economics* 91, Washington, D.C.: Peterson Institute for International Economics, 2010.

Ikeda, Michiko, *Japan in Trade Isolation 1926–37 & 1948–85*, Tokyo, Japan: International House of Japan, Inc., 2008.

Ikeda, Yumi, Monami Yui, and Toru Fujioka, "Japan to Sell $10.4 Billion More Debt to Pay for Earthquake Reconstruction," Bloomberg News Service, October 21, 2011. As of January 18, 2012:
http://mobile.bloomberg.com/news/2011-10-21/japan-to-sell-800-billion-yen-more-debt

IMF—*See* International Monetary Fund.

International Monetary Fund, *Global Financial Stability Report: Grappling with Crisis Legacies*, September 2011. As of November 14, 2011:
http://www.imf.org/External/Pubs/FT/GFSR/2011/02/index.htm#tablesc1

Ito, Aki, and Christopher Anstey, "Moody's Japan Debt Downgrade Clashes with S&P in U.S.," Bloomberg News Service, August 24, 2011. As of 18 January 18, 2012:
http://www.bloomberg.com/news/2011-08-24/moody-s-japan-downgrade-clashes-with-s-p-in-u-s-as-jgbs-steady.html

Ito, Aki, and Keiko Ujikane, "Japan Rating Outlook Lowered to Negative by S&P on Quake Rebuilding Costs," Bloomberg News Service, April 27, 2011. As of October 31, 2011:
http://www.bloomberg.com/news/print/2011-04-27/japan-debt-outlook-cut-to-negative-by-s-p-as-quake-rebuilding-adds-to-debt.html

Jackson, James K., "Trade Agreements: Impact on the U.S. Economy," CRS Report for Congress,  Report No. RL31932, November 10, 2009. As of November 14, 2011:
http://fpc.state.gov/documents/organization/134272.pdf

Jackson, John H., *The World Trading System: Law and Policy of International Economic Relations*, 3rd ed., Cambridge, Mass.: MIT Press, 1997.

Japan Statistics Bureau, Statistical Handbook of Japan 2010, 2011. As of November 14, 2011: http://www.stat.go.jp/english/data/nenkan/1431-03.htm

"Japan's Trade Balance: Seeing Red," *The Economist*, January 14, 2012. As of February 5, 2012: http://www.economist.com/node/21542794

Kimura, F., and A. Kuno, [Evaluation of Japan's EPA Trade Liberalization Level], Keio University KUMQRP Discussion Paper Series 2007-002, 2007.

Kono, Yohei, "Myth and Reality: Why Japan Strives for Multilateralism," speech by the Minister of Foreign Affairs, January 2001. As of November 14, 2011: http://www.mofa.go.jp/announce/fm/kono/speech0101.html

Krauss, Ellis S., and Megumi Naoi, "The Domestic Politics of Japan's Regional Foreign Economic Policies," in V. K. Aggarwal and S. Lee, eds., *Trade Policy in the Asia Pacific: The Role of Ideas, Interests, and Domestic Institutions*, Amsterdam: Springer, 2011.

Lawrence, Robert Z., "Recent Free Trade Initiatives in the Middle East: Opportunities But No Guarantees," Harvard JFK School of Government Faculty Research Working Paper No. RWP06-050, December 2006.

Lincoln, Edward J., "Arthritic Japan: The Slow Pace of Economic Reform," Japan Policy Research Institute Working Paper No. 81, October 2001.

Lord, Arthur, "Demystifying FTAs: A Comparative Analysis of American, Japanese, and Chinese Efforts to Shape the Future of Free Trade," Edwin O. Reischauer Center for East Asian Studies, Asia-Pacific Policy Papers Series, No. 11, 2010.

Ma, Tieying, *Japan: Reconstruction, Growth and Public Debt*, DBS Group Research, December 1, 2011. As of January 18, 2012: https://www.dbsvresearch.com/research/DBS/research.nsf/%28vwAllDocs%29/DD8DD9A38FC6A818425759590019937D/$FILE/jp_20111201.pdf

McLannahan, Ben, "Japanese Debt Appeals to Foreigners," *Financial Times,* January 11, 2012. As of January 18, 2012: http://www.ft.com/intl/cms/s/0/24076ef8-3c30-11e1-8d38-00144feabdc0.html#axzz1leAnImIe

METI—*See* Ministry of Economy, Trade and Industry.

Ministry of Economy, Trade and Industry, "Trends in Overseas Subsidiaries July–September 2011," 2011. As of February 2, 2012: http://www.meti.go.jp/english/statistics/tyo/genntihou/pdf/h2c3l2ye.pdf

Ministry of Finance, "Trade Statistics: Value of Imports and Exports, Calendar Year 2011," released January 30, 2012. As of February 1, 2012: http://www.customs.go.jp/toukei/shinbun/trade-st_e/2011/2011_115e.pdf

Ministry of Foreign Affairs, "Basic Policy on Comprehensive Economic Partnerships," November 6, 2010. As of February 5, 2012: http://www.mofa.go.jp/policy/economy/fta/policy20101106.html

———, "Free Trade Agreement (FTA) and Economic Partnership Agreement (EPA)," 2012. As of February 2, 2012: http://www.mofa.go.jp/policy/economy/fta/index.html

MoFA—*See* Ministry of Foreign Affairs.

Momani, Bessma, "A Middle East Free Trade Area: Economic Interdependence and Peace Reconsidered," *The World Economy*, Vol. 30, No. 11, 2007, pp. 1682–1700.

Mumme, Stephen P., "NAFTA and Environment," Washington, D.C.: Foreign Policy in Focus, October 1, 1999.

Naoi, Megumi, and Ikuo Kume, "Explaining Mass Support for Agricultural Protectionism: Evidence from a Survey Experiment During the Global Recession," paper prepared for a conference on Politics in the New Hard Times in Honor of Peter Gourevitch, University of California, San Diego, April 23–24, 2010.

Neu, C. Richard, and Charles Wolf, Jr., *The Economic Dimensions of National Security*, Santa Monica, Calif.: RAND Corporation, MR-466-OSD, 1994. As of February 2, 2012:
http://www.rand.org/pubs/monograph_reports/MR466.html

OECD—See Organisation for Economic Co-operation and Development.

Organisation for Economic Co-operation and Development, *Agricultural Policy Monitoring and Evaluation 2011: OECD Countries and Emerging Economies*, Paris: OECD Publications, 2011.

———, "Labor Productivity Levels in the Total Economy," *OECD StatExtracts*, 2012. As of January 18, 2012:
http://stats.oecd.org/Index.aspx?DataSetCode=LEVEL

Pang, Eul-Soo, "Embedding Security into Free Trade: The Case of the United States-Singapore Free Trade Agreement," *Contemporary Southeast Asia*, Vol. 29, No. 1, 2007, pp. 1–32.

Park, Yung Chul, Shujiro Urata, and Inkyo Cheong, "The Political Economy of the Proliferation of FTAs," Korea Economic Research Institute Major Research Paper 2005-13, 2005.

Pekkanen, Saadia M., "Bilateralism, Multilateralism, or Regionalism? Japan's Trade Forum Choices," *Journal of East Asian Studies*, Vol. 5, 2005, pp. 77–103.

Pugatch, Meir Perez, "A Transatlantic Divide? The U.S. and EU's Approach to the International Regulation of Intellectual Property Trade-Related Agreements," ECIPE Working Paper No. 2, 2007.

Rodrik, Dani, *Has Globalization Gone Too Far?* Washington, D.C.: Institute for International Economics, 1997.

Rosen, Howard, "Free Trade Agreements as Foreign Policy Tools: The U.S.-Israel and U.S.-Jordan FTAs," in J. J. Schott, ed., *Free Trade Agreements: U.S. Strategies and Priorities*, Washington, D.C.: Institute for International Economics, 2004.

Roy, Martin, Juan Marchetti, and Hoe Lim, "Services Liberalization in the New Generation of Preferential Trade Agreements (PTAs): How Much Further Than the GATS?" WTO Economic Research and Statistics Division Working Paper ERSD-2006-07, Geneva, Switzerland: WTO, 2006.

Rummel, John, "Unions Differ on Korea Trade Pact," *People's World*, December 16, 2010. As of November 14, 2011:
http://peoplesworld.org/unions-differ-on-korea-trade-pact/

Sato, Takafumi, "Global Financial Crisis: Japan's Experience and Policy Response," Remarks presented at the Federal Reserve Bank of San Francisco's Asia Economic Policy Conference in Santa Barbara, California, October 20, 2009.

Schott, Jeffrey J., "Assessing U.S. FTA Policy," in J. J. Schott, ed., *Free Trade Agreements: U.S. Strategies and Priorities,* Washington, D.C.: Institute for International Economics, 2004.

Siracusa, Joseph M., "John Howard, Australia, and the Coalition of the Willing," *Yale Journal of International Affairs*, Winter–Spring 2006, pp. 39–49.

Smith, Carolyn C., "Trade Promotion Authority and Fast-Track Negotiating Authority for Trade Agreements: Major Votes," CRS Report for Congress, No. RS21004, Congressional Research Service, November 2007.

Tiemann, Mary, "NAFTA: Related Environmental Issues and Initiatives," U.S. State Department, Environmental and Natural Resources Policy Division, March 2000. As of June 28, 2011:
http://fpc.state.gov/6143.htm

"Tsunami Risk to Japan's Self-Sufficiency in Rice," *AgriMoney.com*, March 17, 2011. As of January 18, 2012:
http://www.agrimoney.com/news/tsunami-risk-to-japans-self-sufficiency-in-rice--2941.html

United Nations, Economic and Social Survey of Asia and the Pacific, *Sustaining Dynamism and Social Development: Connectivity in the Region and Productive Capacity in Least Developed Countries,* Geneva, 2011.

Urata, Shujiro, "The Emergence and Proliferation of Free Trade Agreements in East Asia," *The Japanese Economy*, Vol. 32, No. 2, Summer 2004, pp. 5–52.

———, "Free Trade Agreements: A Catalyst for Japan's Economic Revitalization," in T. Ito, H. Patrick, and D. E. Weinstein, eds., *Reviving Japan's Economy*, Cambridge, Mass.: The MIT Press, 2005, pp. 377–410.

———, "Japan's New Trade Policy: From GATT and the WTO to FTAs," Waseda University Global Institute for Asian Regional Integration Working Paper 2010-E-8, 31 March 2011. As of November 14, 2011: http://www.waseda-giari.jp/sysimg/imgs/wp2010_e8.pdf

U.S. Bureau of Economic Analysis, "Foreign Direct Investment in the United States: Selected Items by Detailed Industry of U.S. Affiliate,  2007–2010," undated-a. As of February 5, 2012: http://www.bea.gov/international/xls/Long%20Industry%202007-2010.xls

———, "Gross-Domestic-Product-by-Industry Data, Value-Added by Industry, 1998–2010 NAICS Data," undated-b. As of February 5, 2012: http://www.bea.gov/industry/gdpbyind_data.htm

U.S. Census Bureau, "Exports, Imports and Trade Balance by Country, Monthly Totals, 1985–Present," 2012. As of February 5, 2012: http://www.census.gov/foreign-trade/statistics/country/

U.S. Department of Labor, Bureau of Labor Statistics, "Employees on Nonfarm Payrolls by Industry Sector and Selected Industry Detail," February 2012. As of February 5, 2012: http://www.bls.gov/news.release/empsit.t17.htm

U.S. Energy Information Administration, Department of Energy, *Country Analysis Briefs: Japan*, March 2011. As of January 18, 2012: http://205.254.135.7/EMEU/cabs/Japan/pdf.pdf

USGAO—See U.S. Government Accountability Office.

U.S. Government Accountability Office, *An Analysis of Free Trade Agreements and Congressional and Private Sector Consultations under Trade Promotion Authority*, GAO-08-59, December 7, 2007.

USITA—*See* U.S. International Trade Administration.

U.S. International Trade Administration, "U.S. Trade Overview," June 24, 2011. As of February 1, 2012: http://trade.gov/mas/ian/build/groups/public/@tg_ian/documents/webcontent/tg_ian_002065.pdf

USTR—*See* U.S. Trade Representative.

U.S. Trade Representative, undated. As of February 1, 2011: http://www.ustr.gov/trade-agreements/free-trade-agreements

———, "Outlines of the Trans-Pacific Partnership Agreement," November 2011. As of January 18, 2012: http://www.ustr.gov/about-us/press-office/fact-sheets/2011/november/outlines-trans-pacific-partnership-agreement

"Weak Euro Puts Exporters in 'Critical Situation,'" *Asahi Shimbun*, January 17, 2012. As of January 18, 2012: http://ajw.asahi.com/article/economy/AJ201201170053

Williscroft, Colin, "TPP Stepping Stone to More Trade Agreements—Key," *National Business Review New Zealand*, July 22, 2011.

World Bank, *World Development Indicators*, 2011. As of February 1, 2012: http://data.worldbank.org/data-catalog/world-development-indicators

World Trade Organization, *Trade Policy Review of Japan, 2011*, Geneva, Switzerland: WTO, 2011.

———, *Trade Policy Review of the United States, 2010*, Geneva, Switzerland: WTO, 2010a.

———, *Understanding the WTO*, Geneva, Switzerland: WTO, 2010b.

WTO—*See* World Trade Organization.

Zhang, Yunling, and Minghui Shen, "The Status of East Asian free Trade Agreements," Asian Development Bank Institute Working Paper No. 282, May 2011.